REF.
741.60285
C738
1993
D1123965

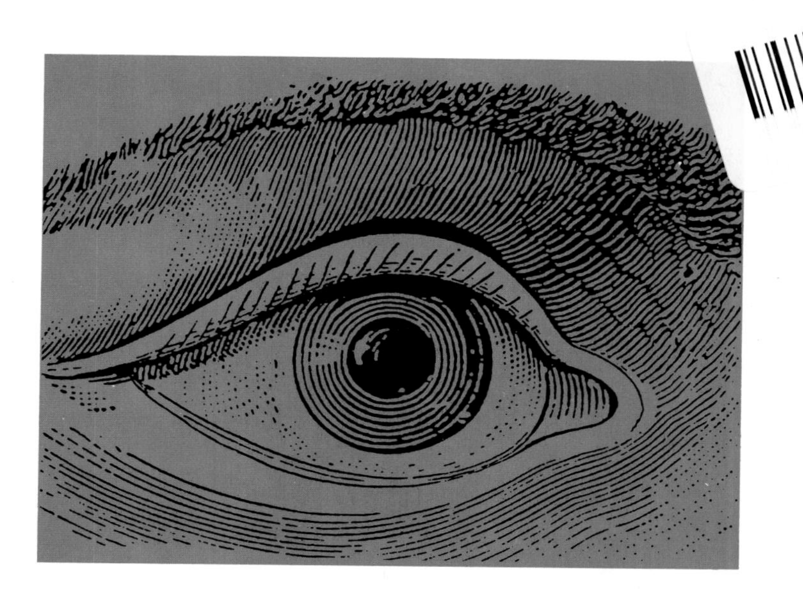

Art Center College of Design
Library
1700 Lida Street
Pasadena, Calif. 91103

To the Children of a New Generation

I thank all featured designers for sharing their time and materials. Thanks to Jack Anderson and Clement Mok for their insight. Also special thanks to the staff at Supon Design Group — Andy, Anthony, Dianne, Rick, Tony, and Wayne — who helped realize this book's smooth completion; to Linda Klinger for her writing; and to Henry Kornman for his wisdom.

For Reference
Not to be taken
from this library

ART CENTER COLLEGE OF DESIGN
3 3220 00129 7238

COMPUTER GENERATION

How Designers View Today's Technology

Art Center College of Design
Library
1700 Lida Street
Pasadena, Calif. 91103

With comment
by Jack Ander
of Hornall And
Design Works,
Clement Mok,
Clement Mok

Supon Design Group

Copyright 1993

by Supon Design Group, Inc.,
International Book Divison

All rights reserved. Copyright under International and Pan-American Copyright Conventions.

No part of this book may be reproduced, stored in a retrieval system or transmitted in any other form, or by any means, electronic, mechanical, photocopying, recording or otherwise, without prior permission of the publishers.

While Supon Design Group makes every effort possible to publish full and correct credits for each work included in this volume, sometimes errors of omission or commission may occur. For this we are most regretful, but hereby must disclaim any liability.

As this book is printed in four-color process, a few of the designs reproduced here may appear to be slightly different than in their original reproduction.

Distributed to the trade in the United States, Canada and Mexico by:

Books Nippan
1123 Dominguez Street, Unit K
Carson, CA 90746
Fax: (310) 604-1134

Distributed throughout the rest of the world by:

Nippon Shuppan Hanbai Inc.
3-4 Chome Kandasurugadai, Chiyoda-ku
Tokyo 101, Japan
Fax: (03) 3233-1578

Publisher:

Nippan Publications
1123 Dominguez Street, Unit K
Carson, CA 90746

Computer Generation is a project of:

Supon Design Group, Inc., International Book Division
1000 Connecticut Avenue, NW, Suite 415
Washington, DC 20036
(202) 822-6540

Printed in Hong Kong
ISBN 0-945814-23-2
Library of Congress Catalog Card Number 93-084507

Acknowledgments

Project Director
Supon Phornirunlit

Communications Director
Wayne Kurie

Art Director and Editor
Supon Phornirunlit

Managing Editor
Wayne Kurie

Book Designer
Dianne S. Cook

Cover Designer
Richard Lee Heffner

Writers
Linda Klinger
Wayne Kurie

Staff
Andrew Dolan
Anthony Michael Fletcher
Betty Hong
Tony Wilkerson

Production Assistant
Jennifer A. Lowe

Desktop Publishing
CompuPrint, Washington, D.C.

CONTENTS

Introduction

Commentaries

Art Center College of Design
Library
1700 Lida Street
Pasadena, Calif. 91103

Studios

INTRODUCTION

It was in the early 1980s that the union of machinery and craftwork became an acceptable and affordable tool for change in the design field. Back then, it was compared to the Industrial Revolution — a 20th-century upheaval that infused chips, grids, and flat screens into the graphic world of color, textured paper, and intuition. Computers and commercial art — now that they're consolidated, how critical is their influence to the evolution of design? Are computers synthesizing technology and art, or creating a new, stereotypical style?

Computer Generation represents a dialogue of worldwide designers who are rethinking the role of computers in the studio. The value of the tool is apparent, but what's unknown and consistently debated is the direction in which it will eventually take the industry. From this uncertainty comes the question: what do the terms "technology," "graphic design," and "designer" really mean? Defining these terms has changed the perception of graphic art. Some designers believe in the computer's singular creative value, while others see it only as a means to an end.

In writing this book, we heard from those who perceived that computer use would dissolve creativity into machine-rendered solutions. That is one definition of "technology," and others include engineering, mass-production, assembly lines, or even a pencil. Because of the industrial connotations that can intrude on a world that borders — if not encompasses — the aesthetic, some say technology should be reserved for supporting no-frills business objectives, like accounting, rather than used to execute a tried-and-true design method a little crisper, a little straighter, or a little faster. The flaws themselves, say some, have value.

The term "graphic design" is usually defined as a form of public aesthetic — a fusion of business language and creativity. The computer has been accused of changing the business of design by siphoning the "art" from "graphic art." But is design an extension of artwork, or a form of marketing and communication using colors and lines?

Consider the third component — the designer. Called a computer operator in some studios, many question whether a computer can make a "hacker" into an artist. If a computer can make poor work look like real commercial art to the untrained eye, won't computers open the door to graphics jobs for desktop-publishers as well as designers, and perhaps flood the market with low-quality work? Some laud the power of technology as a boost to designers who pursue graphics as a means to make money, not because of a strong interest or commitment in art or design. But is this good or bad?

Technology is also the impetus for a new valuation of graphic skills: a designer's familiarity with Macintosh, Quark XPress, and PageMaker rate at the top of the list of skills highly regarded by many potential clients or employers. And what about the merit of drawing skills, the ability to illustrate, or create type? Are we in danger of losing these skills? When does the designer cross the line and become a technician, and who is "more creative?"

Some clients now expect designers to be expert in prepress, stripping, typography, and high-resolution scanning — which are crafts in themselves. Designers who use computers to accomplish these tasks have already put some of the craft masters out of business. More and more often, a machine appears to have realigned the traditional relationship between studio and client by blurring the lines between designer and a multitude of specific trade services and skills.

These observations are troubling to some designers, but the lure of speed and economy via technology is irresistable to most. There are still challenges in making the transition to computer-generated design, however, and most are addressed by the studios included here. The common hurdles: high cost; lengthy learning curve; design similarity due to the volume of work being produced and the limited software programs; new in-house responsibilities for proofreading; kerning, trapping, and color fidelity that need special attention; and quality reduction — computers make it easier to do bad design quickly and within budget. Industry analysts note increased graphic density without improved meaning, and a loss of personality directly resulting from a gain in technological tricks and gimmicks.

There are, of course, benefits, or computers would have long since gone the way of all trends. More speed, of course. Studios can generate their own type and manipulate it endlessly. There is color on demand. Through the careful infusion of technology into handwork without compromising identity, we know it is possible to become a legacy in computer design, and we've included a few of the legends here. And computers have given new independence to studios as one-stop shops for most client graphic needs, affording them total control of the product.

And the Incredible Results Speak for Themselves

When we asked about the future role of computers in design, we heard enthusiasm mixed with caution. The process is high quality, but not yet perfect. There are alliances to be forged between programers and designers frustrated by today's software limitations. The computer will not soon be a tool for all seasons. But most designers agree: what you get out of it depends on what you put into it, supported or detracted by your desire for change. The discussion goes on. This book is presented as an addition to that discussion, not a conclusion.

At Supon Design Group, we recognize the value of technology in our projects. But we value more the thought processes that precede computer incorporation. As this book showed us, there is always something to be learned. Designers are using computers in ways we never considered. This book offers a perspective on the state of design today, and can be used to make predictions as to its direction tomorrow.

But, overall, we agree with psychologist B.F. Skinner: "The real problem is not whether machines think, but whether people do."

Supon Phornirunlit is owner of Supon Design Group, Inc., where he serves as creative director and art director. He founded the company in 1988, and since, he and his design team have earned over 300 awards, including recognition from every major national design competition. Supon Design Group's work has appeared in publications such as Graphis, Communication Arts, Print, Studio, *and* HOW. *He and his studio have been profiled in many publications. Supon has appeared on cable television's "Alexandria Journal" program, and was a guest on Asian radio. He regularly speaks at various organizations and schools.*

COMMENTARY

by Clement Mok

I have been asked to write about design and computers for a number of years now. My views about the subject change as technology continues to change — any evaluation is merely a snapshot of prevailing thoughts and trends. Changes are often dramatic and consequences are impossible to predict. The only certainty is that there are more changes to come, and at an increasing pace.

My opinions might differ, but my perspective has not; it is still the perspective of a graphic designer. During the last 10 years of my professional career, I've been part of the microcomputing industry — and its ups and downs. I have worked with many of the techno-gurus and assisted the birth of new products. These experiences gave me a unique if not privileged perspective. The thoughts expressed here are based on both personal experience and conversations with designers, writers, and engineers around the country.

About four years ago, I came across an article that quoted Milton Glaser on his views about computers. It read: "The battle with the computer is over. They've won. The losses have yet to be counted."

As a humanist, I couldn't agree with him more, but that is as far as I am willing to go along with his battle cry — a cry to return to a world that's simpler, slower, and more mystical, a world that has regional and cultural differences providing a beacon for one's own identity. This sentiment and theme have been echoed universally time and time again throughout modern history, starting from the Industrial Age — this grief and sense of loss is what makes us beings "human."

We are part of a natural order poised in a state of delicate equilibrium, safe as long as we keep to our position within it. The "natural order" is very basic. It is the principle that you cannot have something for nothing, everything has its price, nothing in life is free, or there can be no gain without pain. Technologists, in their zest to invent a better mousetrap, have forgotten about this natural order. In their zeal to provide us with improved tools in the name of progress, we are thrust into a world of rapid changes demanding behavior modifications that took a lifetime to develop. No one bothered to tell us — or to figure out — what we are giving up.

The Losses Are Plenty, But So Are the Gains

Our business is about ideas and their implementation. There's not a shortage of good ideas; only shortages of good, insightful design. Graphic design is a silly title that has little or no meaning these days. Just about anyone who can design can be a graphic designer, and just about anyone can design a newsletter or brochure with a Mac and a laser printer. If not, you can hire the expert on publication design at your local "Instant Printing" store. Anyone can get fonts. Charcoal drawings are available by buying a Photoshop plug-in filter and applying it to a photograph. The things that used to differentiate us from other professions have turned into everyday commodity products. In a sense, the computer is a great equalizer — it allows the most untrained and unskilled to create things that look and smell like design.

The U.S. census tells us there are more people involved with publishing today than at any time in the country's history. Witness the growth of self-help design publications over the last five years. *How* and *Step-by-Step* both have circulations higher than *Print, Communication Arts, ID,* or *Graphis.* Who are all these people?

Everyone is a designer — including our clients. Do we as professional designers differentiate ourselves by our ability to use graphic software? You may laugh, but in many cases, that's what's going on out there. When the things our clients can create look and smell like design, the pressure is on us to articulate and demonstrate what we can bring to the table, even if it means changing what we create. It's not enough to say we solve communication problems — so can a telephone operator.

The profession I entered 15 years ago is so very different than the one I am in now. Look at the careers of Paul Rand, George Tchierny, Bradbury Thompson, Ivan Chermayeff, Lou Dorfsman. Graphic design was supposed to be a life-long career. How wrong could I possibly have been? Tools have changed dramatically and will continue to do so, with great momentum. But we are not the only ones puzzled by what's going on around us. Advertising agencies, photographers, lawyers, accountants — anyone and everyone related to the service sector has and will be affected by the advent of these new emerging technologies.

New Realities

The world we once knew as being so infinite has forever changed. The industries of computing, television, and telecommunications are blending into one. The products that will be introduced in the coming years will certainly erase what we understand the boundaries between computers and television to be. These shifts are sweeping the way we interact with computers and what we do with these new gadgets. Computers will help users manage information with agents that will simplify tasks that now take a great deal of human intervention. Rule-based design will be replaced by these computer agents, animation by virtual reality, pen by voice and gesture.

We have new forms of information storage and retrieval that will allow us the ability to access computer information anywhere, anytime. The key might be cellular, hand-held devices that use radio waves to span miles.

Our workday is 24 hours long — or short. Voice mail messages can be left at all hours. Shipped packages arrive overnight — faxes, in minutes. Scanning replaces reading. Channel-zapping replaces TV-watching. Every message is simplified and shrunk into news bits, factoids, and soundbites. Nobody, least of all the consumer of our well-designed information, wants to wait. The things we design will have to be bolder, shorter, and simpler just to get people's attention. Images will be either predigested or non-sequitur. Some combinations already exist today: home shopping networks, on-demand publishing at various copy centers, Fax or multi-media mail publishing, interactive digital books and magazines, interactive broadcast or receiver-centered publishing. There will be others.

In 1990, I heard Paul Saffo speak at the AIGA conference in San Antonio, and what he said stayed with me: "Technology has always changed the way we experience the world. And, therefore, the way we design and create. And, ultimately, the things we design and create."

The possibilities are there if you look for them. Happy Hunting.

Clement Mok's experience spans a broad range of media including print, video, computer-based multimedia, environmental design, and event marketing. Prior to forming his own agency, he was creative director at Apple Computer, where he directed a myriad of projects, including the launch of the Macintosh. As founder and creative director of Clement Mok Designs (San Francisco, California, USA), Mok oversees all design and product development. His experience in the computing industry and his expertise with new media has prompted numerous technology companies to invite him to serve on their boards. His work has been widely published and has received over 100 awards. Mok's designs have also been exhibited in museums and galleries in Europe and Japan.

Almost everyone has said it before: "The computer doesn't design. It's only a tool." Yet it still amazes me the discipline required to avoid picking up this computer tool prematurely. Tissue pads or the back of an envelope still seem to me to be the preferred media to create the best, freshest, rule-breaking ideas.

While technology has found a secure place in our studio, members of our staff still engage in other exploration: spinning a piece of line art on a copy machine, rubbing a texture through soft paper, splattering paint through a movable stencil, scanning images and tranferring them to acetate, or layering-over patterns. These are the global thinkers, the detail people. Hornall Anderson also has those who see solutions entirely through the computer — people who execute production services through technology. Occasionally, we find someone who can do both, but it's rare. We work very hard to build project teams with both computer technicians and brush-in-hand designers. The mix of different mediums produces the most interesting solutions.

I am a self-confessed, ineffectual computer operator. It's a condition that grew a little out of laziness, but mostly by choice — I chose to concentrate on concepts rather than execution. Too many other commitments and the computer's steep learning curve still prevent me from becoming a hardware and software expert. Although I'm fascinated by computer potential and plan on taking my place among the computer-literate eventually, today, I admit my comfort at the keyboard is less than blissful.

Not so with our design staff. Clearly, the firm of Hornall Anderson is part of the "computer generation." We do, however, continuously discuss and debate the role that the computer should play in our design process. Without exception, we all see the value in — and have been seduced by — the speed and the degree of finish the computer brings to the mix: the tighter comps, range of color, composition studies, the efficiency. Knowing when to turn the computer off is the trick. A half-baked, weak concept only becomes a tight, well-comp'd, half-baked, weak concept if you jump into the box too soon.

New Challenges

Despite its allure, the computer nas also challenged us in several arenas, the most critical of which include liability and accountability, appropriate compensation and overhead investments, and avoiding a stylized look.

One of the greatest impacts on our business has been a new accountablity. As we create more and more of our jobs electronically, we assume increased liability in the areas of typesetting and prepress. Proofreading and stripping errors join lost transparencies on our growing list of business fears.

Not so long ago, someone else was responsible for interpreting what we'd written on the board or on the tissue overlay. Today, we do it all — from the simplest projects to the complicated and labor-intensive tasks, like the intricate deck plans for a brochure on a cruise ship. Most of it finds its way onto the disk, and we must pull up expensive new proofs each time we want to accurately check the work. Although clients sign off on proofs, galleys, mechanicals, bluelines, chromalins, and printed sheets, the burden of liability is primarily ours, and a typo or stripping error that slips into the final product will tarnish our relationship with the client.

It's also a challenge to be properly compensated for this new liability. We're still trying to set procedures that will both reimburse us for the savings from prepress and compensate us for the extra hours spent in providing new, in-house services. Today, it's commonplace that designers have become typesetters, then proof-readers — it's no longer a question of whether that will happen, because it already has. But that work had been done by prepress before — and charged to clients accordingly. While we as a studio are assuming the role of heroes to our clients with fast, efficient, and quality design, someone still must pay the cost to avoid mistakes. It's so easy to do in-house what we used to bill as "out-of-pocket expenses" that we have to remind our clients — and ourselves — that we must be reimbursed for the type, the photography, the illustration. Unless the process is properly monitored, clients can get a stylized photo image that's the anchor visual for the entire brochure — for free.

In this aspect and so many others, our studio is a beta site, experimenting with new ways of accomplishing old objectives and charging appropriate fees. It takes an open-minded client to let us do that and share in the responsibility. In addition, many clients have been sold the notion that work is faster and less expensive when done in the magic, one-step, it-can-do-anything box. Quite often, that's not the case.

Self-Assessment

Our value to a client is our ability to problem-solve, to deliver a well-thought-out solution. I prefer those solutions that avoid a trademark "Hornall Anderson look." A look or technique should not be the conceptual platform for an idea. We want the whole breadth of different experiences. One way of achieving this and avoiding becoming stereotypical is to use project teams; another is to regard the computer as only one resource and consistently seek solutions with different tools.

If a client comes to us with a preconceived idea of what role the computer will play in our design process, it can create some problems. Some clients and designers adopt more of a "program process" mentality when they work exclusively with the computer. This program process can limit possibilities for what we call "happy accidents." Some of our most interesting solutions blend electronically generated images with conventionally produced, organic work.

Regardless of the challenges, I often regard a particularly good piece of computer design with envy. For now, I can tell a designer that the piece should have an open feeling, this percent of text, and must sell the product — it's up to him or her to get the orange gradiation precise with the blue and gray line. I look forward to the time when I understand how to operate computers better than I do now, so I can harness more power to interpret my ideas, and easily guide a designer in a new technique he or she should explore.

Computers are so exciting. They can take you almost anywere you want to go. But good ideas can lose their spontaneity because they've been tricked or stylized to death. The wisdom seems to lie in knowing when to quit, to keep from beating the freshness out of the project.

Or perhaps a better example is to compare a computer to a good meal. Know the definition of "enough" — and partake in moderation.

Jack Anderson, one of the founders of Hornall Anderson Design Works (Seattle, Washington, USA), combines design talents with a leadership role in project management. He is experienced in virtually all areas of design: corporate and brand identity, collateral, sporting graphics, packaging, and environmental graphics. His client roster is equally diverse, including international travel and hospitality companies, retailers and distributors, high-technology companies, recreational sport leaders, and more. Anderson's work has repeatedly been recognized in annual competitions and his firm has been profiled in numerous publications. In 1989, Pantone Color Institute named Hornall Anderson Design Works the top graphic design firm of the year.

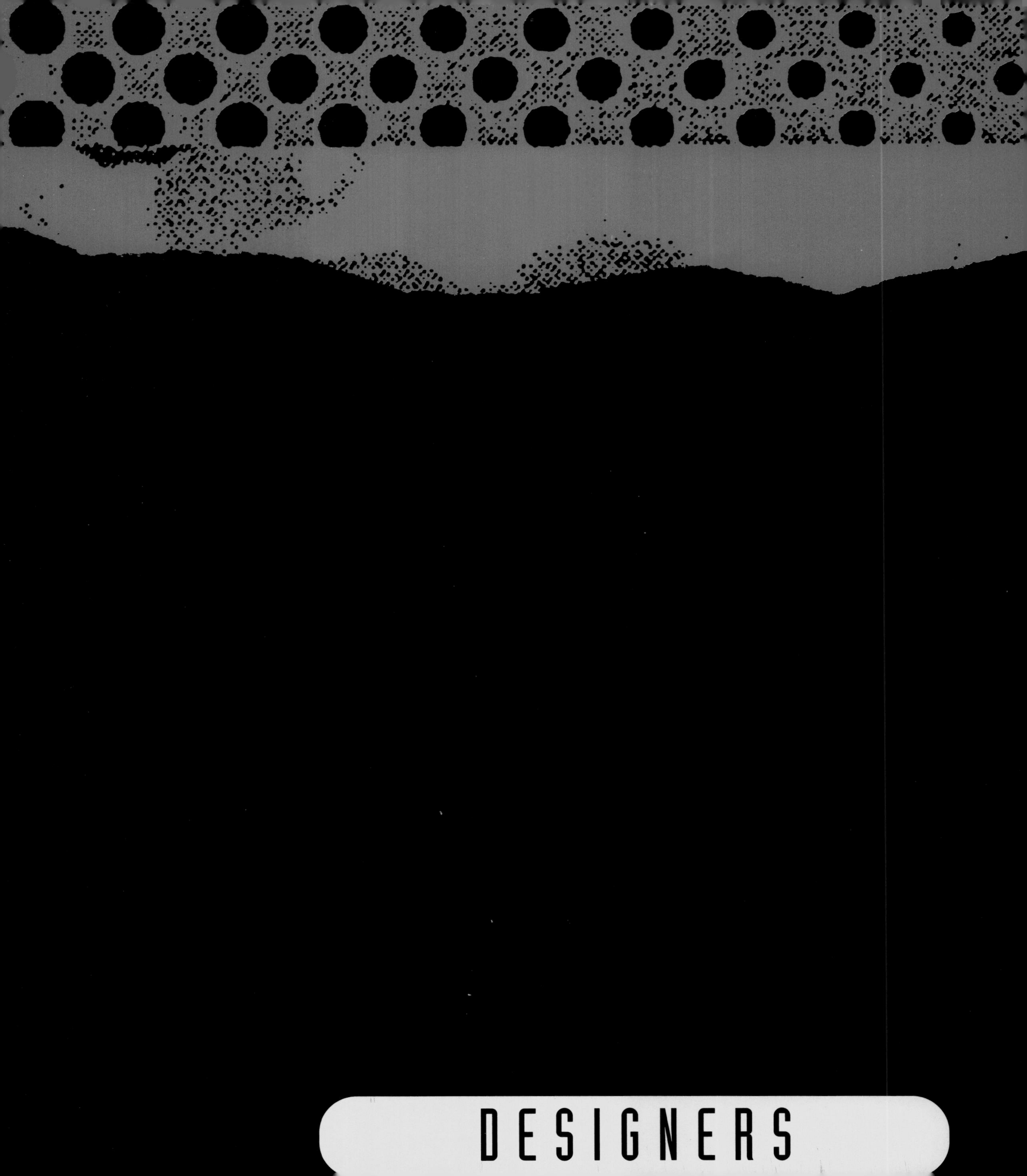

DESIGNERS

April Greiman, Inc.

Los Angeles, California, USA

April Greiman

April Greiman continues to pioneer technology in graphic, environmental, motion, and interactive design. In addition to a recent Hallmark Fellowship, Greiman has been awarded a grant from the National Endowment for the Arts. She has been featured in many magazine articles and on documentary and business programs on PBS, ESPN, and CNN. In 1990, Greiman published the book *Hybrid Imagery — The Fusion of Technology and Graphic Design*. Her work has been the subject of numerous one-woman shows from Tokyo to Jerusalem to New York. Greiman's design is displayed in the permanent collections of the Library of Congress,

IDENTITY SYSTEM

Cerritos Center for the

SIGNAGE SYSTEM
Cerritos Center for the
Performing Arts

TILE MOTIF
Cerritos Center for the
Performing Arts

LIFETIME

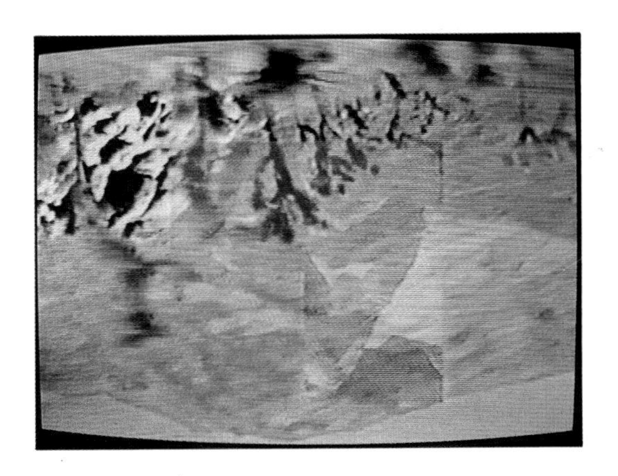

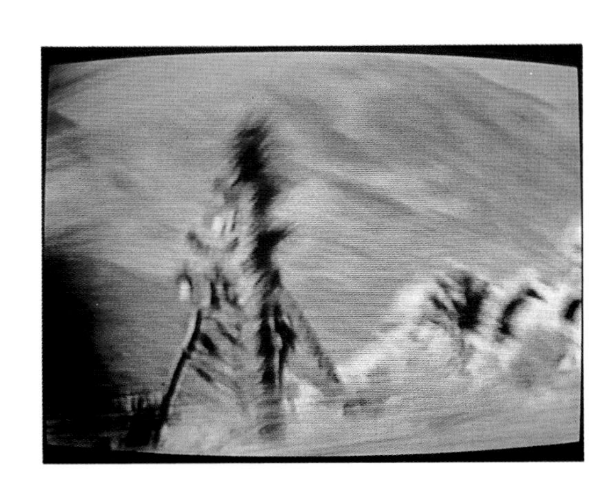

"Graphic design and technology have always been aligned," asserts April Greiman. "The computer process helps us co-create collectively and globally. We are all speaking a new language because of this. Information control is no longer a triangular-type paradigm graphically, from the top down — it's an elliptical or horizontal format of empowerment. People who have mastered technology develop their own visual language within it, and together.

"Our studio started using a computer in 1984 (as a toy) and turned it into our main workhorse. We went through the period when there was so little software available, so when sophisticated programs came out, we spent eight years learning about them as a new aesthetic. We haven't yet scratched the surface of what these programs can do! I haven't played enough yet with black and white and now the color is out! As my friend Eric Martin said, software can be far more interesting than the people using it; all humans are creative, and computers can empower people and assist them to do interesting things. Once you get past the technical part of the learning curve, you're freed up and computers become an incredible intuitive tool.

"Computer design can be cold and impersonal if you're not very good. You become better by exploring. I think many of the other famous designers in this country are about 20 years older than me and have a 'thanks, but I'll stick to my pencil' attitude — an aversion to technology. I suppose I'm the 'bridge generation' — trained traditionally but incorporating computers early in my career. Young designers whose first experience with typography is on the Mac still need traditional role models, like me, to make up for the traditional education in skills which many of them no longer receive. And then, hopefully, they'll pass it on to still younger designers.

"Our studio is bumping its head all the time, not having enough power or memory. The cost is too high. We're not state-of-the-art — we're at the low end, in fact. We have three permanent color workstations and sometimes rent a fourth. We're not into CD ROM and, with limited memory, can only simulate motion graphics. But we're doing what we want to do. Money is directed back into the business, or into people doing creative work.

"Technology's weak link, until recently, was the art of typography. Of course, one still has to have an eye for these things in the first place.

"Creativity is not exclusive to artists; some people do good work regardless of what they call themselves, and some, bad. The computer takes a lot of blame for making things look stupid, but, after all, you can do a stupid thing with a pencil, too!"

Pacific Theater

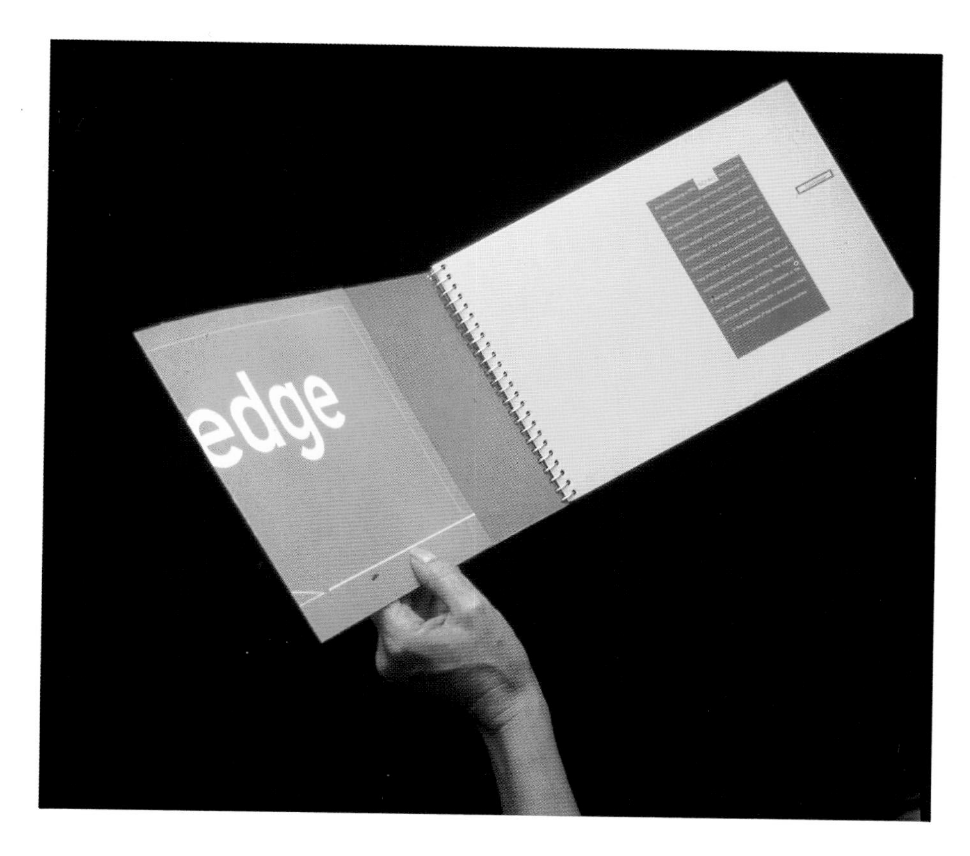

From the Edge

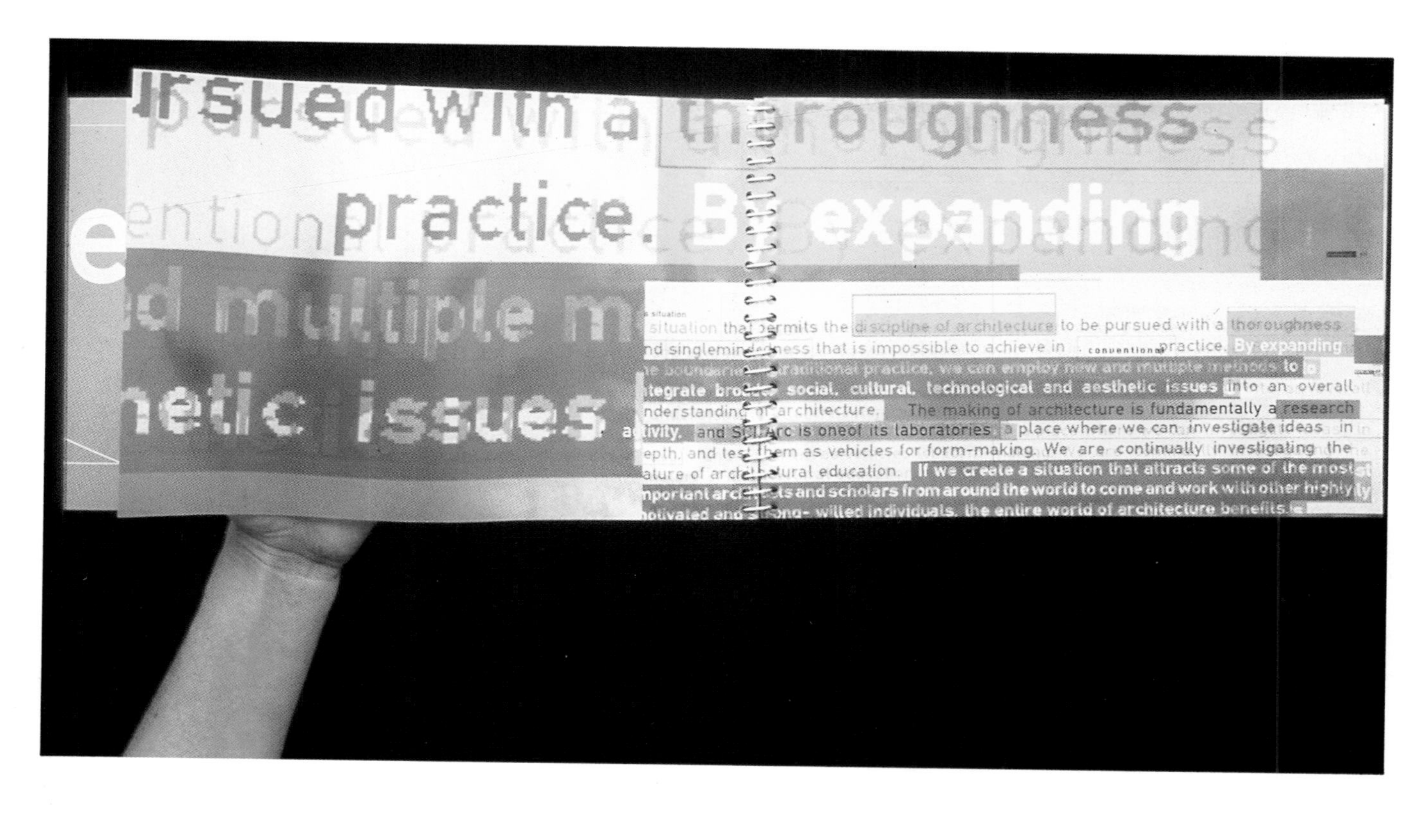

Brigham Young University Graphics

Provo, Utah, USA

McRay Magleby and Bruce Patrick

McRay Magleby, BYU creative director and professor of graphic design at the University of Utah, joined BYU in 1969. He and his staff have earned recognition in publications such as *Graphis, Communication Arts,* and *Creativity. HOW* named him one of the "Twelve Most Influential Designers Today." In 1986, he was appointed Designer of the Decade by the Council for Advancement and Support of Education, and his poster "Wave of Peace" was voted the Most Memorable Poster in the World. Bruce Patrick, art director of BYU's *Brigham Young Magazine,* started his graphics career at BYU in 1985. Patrick also teaches typography and design classes, and has been honored with awards from AIGA and the Art Directors Club of Salt Lake City, among others.

Phoenix

POSTER
Peace

Astronomy compels the soul to look upwards and leads us from this world to another.

BROCHURE
Cryptic Hieroglyphics Spread

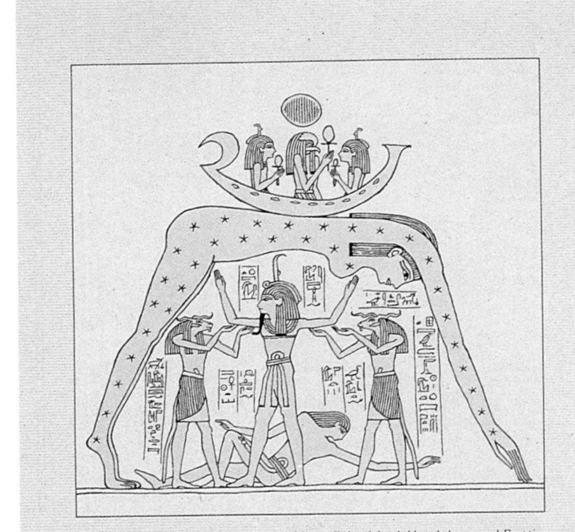

Cryptic hieroglyphics, which have been carefully studied and decoded by scholars, reveal Egyptian reverence and preoccupation with the heavens. In the common mythical drawing depicted here, Nut, the sky-goddess, reclines over the world and is supported by Shu, the god of light and air. Nut gives birth to the sun each day, who travels across her body in a boat. Before 3,000 B.C., Egyptians had ordered their daily activities by fairly accurate calendars based on celestial observations. When the dog star, Sirius, first appeared at dawn on the eastern horizon, farmers knew that the Nile was about to flood. Egyptian engineers also used the heavens to position the great pyramids and temples.

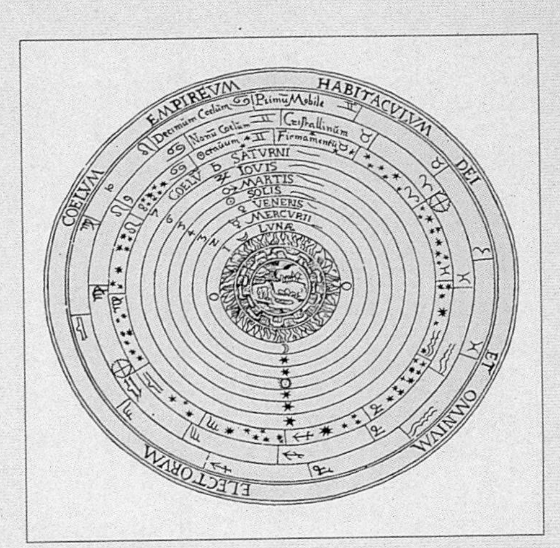

During the fourth century B.C., Aristotle founded his own academy in Athens. There he advanced his far-reaching philosophy about physics and astronomy. Building upon ideas of other great philosophers like Pythagoras, Plato, and Eudoxos, Aristotle formulated models of the universe based on spheres within spheres—layer upon layer like an onion skin. The Greeks, who highly admired harmonious form, marveled at the symmetry of the sphere. The model shown here includes a sphere for the moon, another for the sun, one for each of the five planets, one for the fixed stars, and an outer, invisible sphere, for the prime mover of it all. The spheres above the moon were thought to be eternal and unchanging.

1 2 3 4 5

BROCHURE
Astronomy Spread

BROCHURE
Rembrandt as Printmaker

POSTER
Parrot

The computer, says McRay "Mac" Magleby, is quick to provide a variety of design options, but during critical times, it may slow you down. "You're depending on a device that's difficult to analyze," he says, "and unknown technical difficulties are common."

But Brigham Young University's Graphics department readily admits it uses computers to pioneer new techniques in design. "You learn what caused a problem after the problem is solved," explains art director Bruce Patrick. "Because we strive for unique methods to make our work unexpected, it seems like every job encounters a new challenge." They are constantly pushing the hardware and software beyond all previous limitations.

"We haven't yet found something that can't be translated to the machine, but spontaneity doesn't reproduce well," asserts Magleby, who has watched manual methods, such as airbrushing, phased out over the years. Many of his posters — widely regarded as works of fine art — are sold in galleries that have their own standards. "Some galleries prefer hand-rendering, and hand-crafted quality cannot yet be achieved with computers. The flaws in the line — textures on the edges, imprecision in the width, the way the line is configured — create movement, and make hand-rendering unpredictable. The computer can look predictable."

Magleby and Patrick acknowledge the computer as a valued part of their department. By 1992, there was a computer at each designer's workstation, and almost every project required its use. "Technology is also useful with stock photos," says Patrick. "With a hard disk of 35 images from a stock photo company, we can integrate any one image into a layout. We're also exploring image archival, so that designers can pull an image from the disk or file server without handling the original."

Cerberus

Fish

POSTER
AIDS

Bright & Associates

Venice, California, USA

Keith Bright

Bright & Associates was founded in 1977 by Keith Bright and, today, has offices in the U.S. and Taiwan. Its staff experience includes both domestic and international projects in telecommunications, financial services, food and beverage, travel and entertainment, health and beauty care, sports, and consumer products. Bright's influence can be seen in the development of major corporate identity, packaging, graphic communications, and environmental design programs that include the 1984 Los Angeles Olympics. The firm has received many gold medals and design awards, from AIGA to New York Art Directors Club to the Advertising Club of Los Angeles. Bright's work has appeared in publications worldwide.

PACKAGING

Darkseed Computer Software

Speedway Cafe

Wok Fast

BROCHURES
Yonex Golf & Tennis

MobilWorks

TYPE BOOKS
Andresen Typographics

"Computers have changed this business completely," states Keith Bright of Bright & Associates. "We never predicted this. But now, almost all our work is done on computer."

There's always a computer running at Venice-based Bright & Associates. Nine high-end graphic workstations provide seven designers with instant access to scanning, networking, and color printing technology. In addition, administrative workstations keep the business of business operating smoothly.

Across the world, Bright's Taiwan office, which concentrates on managing a major consulting project for the Government of Taiwan, is equally supported. Four Macintosh stations allow the office to produce in-house materials and maintain overseas contact.

Bright comments on the infusion of computers in his own company: "A few years ago, my graphics staff started using computers," Bright explains. "They motivated me to work with them, and now our business can't do without the equipment. Personally, for an old 'designosaur,' the technology is intimidating. Computers can be difficult to learn and the user manuals aren't much help. I've learned that it's best to stick with what you know — so I let my staff take over at the keyboard.

"If computers have a problem, it's that some people don't know when to stop. Overdesigning is a concern. There are just too many variations available. Some people get stuck in computers. It's easy to get stuck perfecting one design that ends up looking great in the trash. Clients come to us with problems. They don't care if the solution is done on the computer or not."

But Bright respects the infusion of computers in the graphic design workplace, remarking that younger people are at the center of this technological revolution. "They're the key to computer design," states Bright. "Computers give them a chance to experiment, but they must put good ideas and good design first. Only by exploring new techniques can young people continue to improve the quality of their work."

BROCHURE
Resort at Squaw Creek

SHOPPING BAG
Murauchi

MANUAL
Mitsubishi Electronic Division

Bruce Yelaska Design

San Francisco, California, USA

Bruce Yelaska

In 1984, Bruce Yelaska founded his San Francisco design studio after working as a graphic artist at firms in California and Chicago, his hometown. He earned a B.S. degree with honors in Industrial and Graphic Design from the University of Illinois at Chicago. Yelaska is a faculty member at the University of California at Berkeley, where he teaches part-time and has developed design symposiums with world-renowned designers. He has written several articles for industry publications. His client list includes such diverse organizations as WTTW Chicago, Ralston Purina, Apple Computer Company, and Levi Strauss & Co.

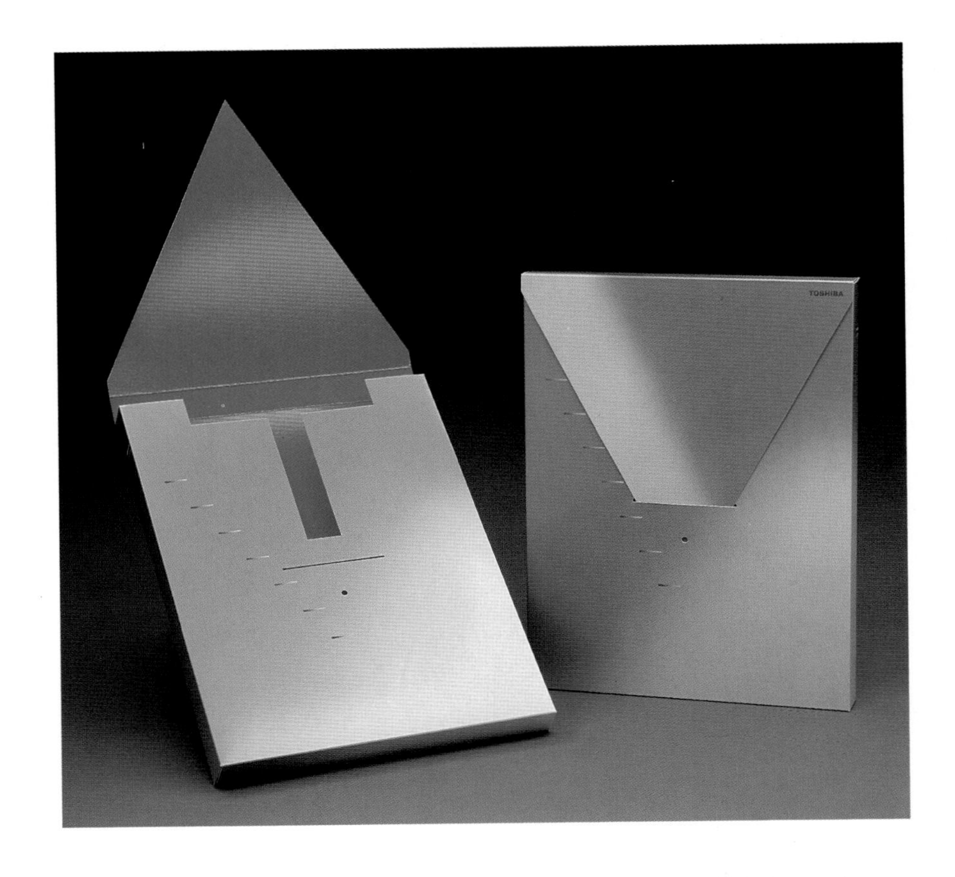

Toshiba MRI

Catalyst

Catalyst

HORSE

Urban Horse

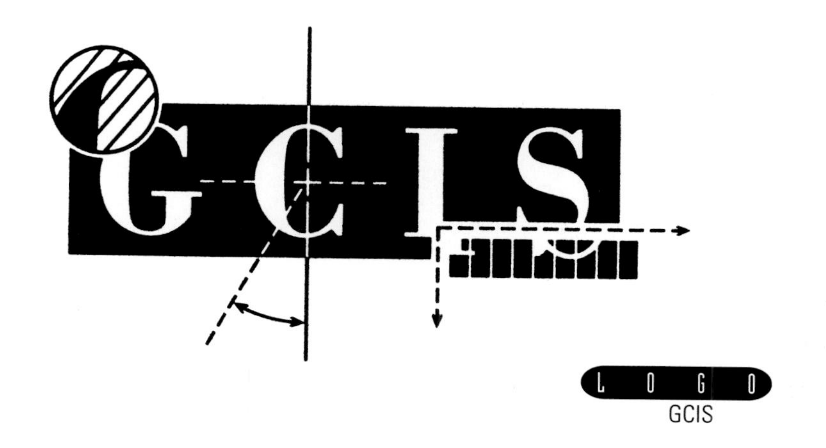

LOGO
GCIS

Cafe Toma

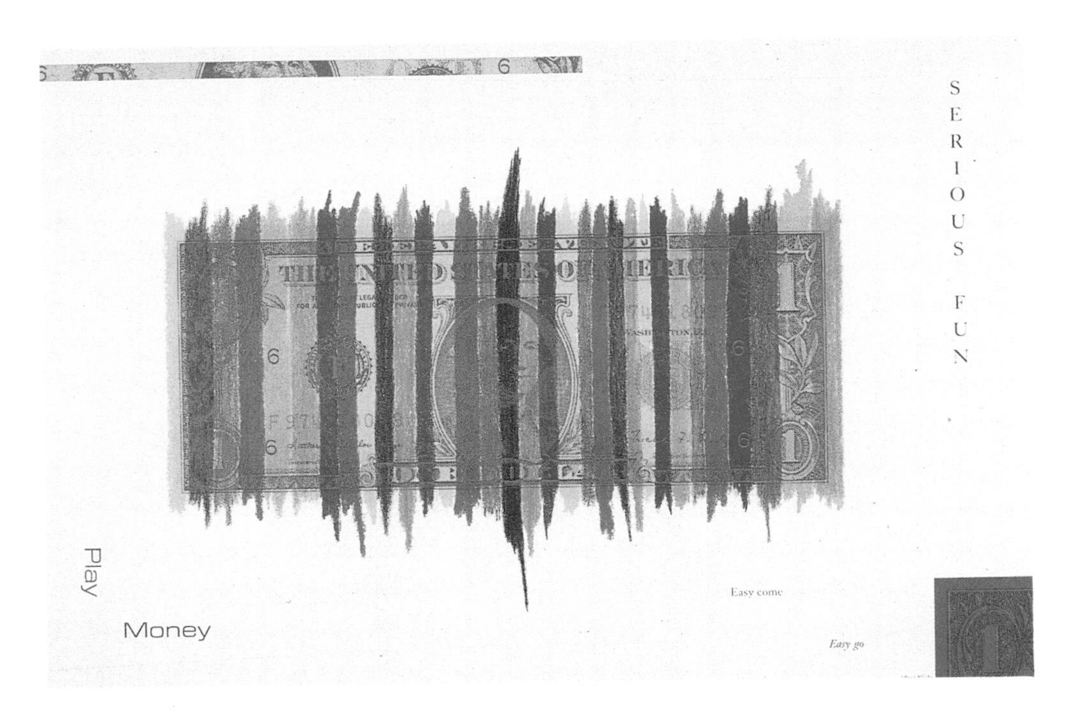

Serious Fun

Life on Earth

Rethinking the Future

Life on Earth

Life on Earth

"You must know what design is before deciding what technology to implement," maintains Bruce Yelaska, who uses computers for about one-third of his tasks. "A computer will never design on its own. But it will make you think you're a designer. Invent the design first, then choose the media to execute it.

"Designers must not bypass components of a design education with technology. Don't let the project be technology-driven rather than design-driven. If you use the computer improperly, the art becomes just a technique. It's odd that we're all supposed to be so creative, but almost all designers who use computers use only one type of hardware and two programs." But, "Some jobs are too massive not to use computers," he admits, citing a contract for a 500-page book he produces twice a year that requires electronic intervention.

Because of its speed, Yelaska concedes that the computer has saved money in certain areas of production. "If the client, for example, wants 10 logos on a logo sheet in different sizes, or wants to adjust the artwork, it can be done in minutes. Of course, we're constantly upgrading our equipment as our jobs require it, buying additional memory and so on. But eventually we'll have the completed system we need."

His studio employs two full-time designers, two part-timers, and has only one workstation. But a single computer is not a problem; Yelaska emphasizes thinking first and integrating the computer later. "Because computers have an almost infinite amount of capability, you can make an infinite amount of time-consuming changes if you don't think the problem through beforehand."

Yelaska teaches design at University of California at Berkeley. "Students in my introductory classes cannot use the computer at all. I want them to think about what they're doing. It's so easy to make changes on the computer that you can make a lot of adjustments to a mediocre idea. First, you must decide if the idea works. If it's not a good idea, it won't work, no matter where you move it on the page."

TOILET SEAT
Your Future Has Past

BROCHURE
Kohnke Printing

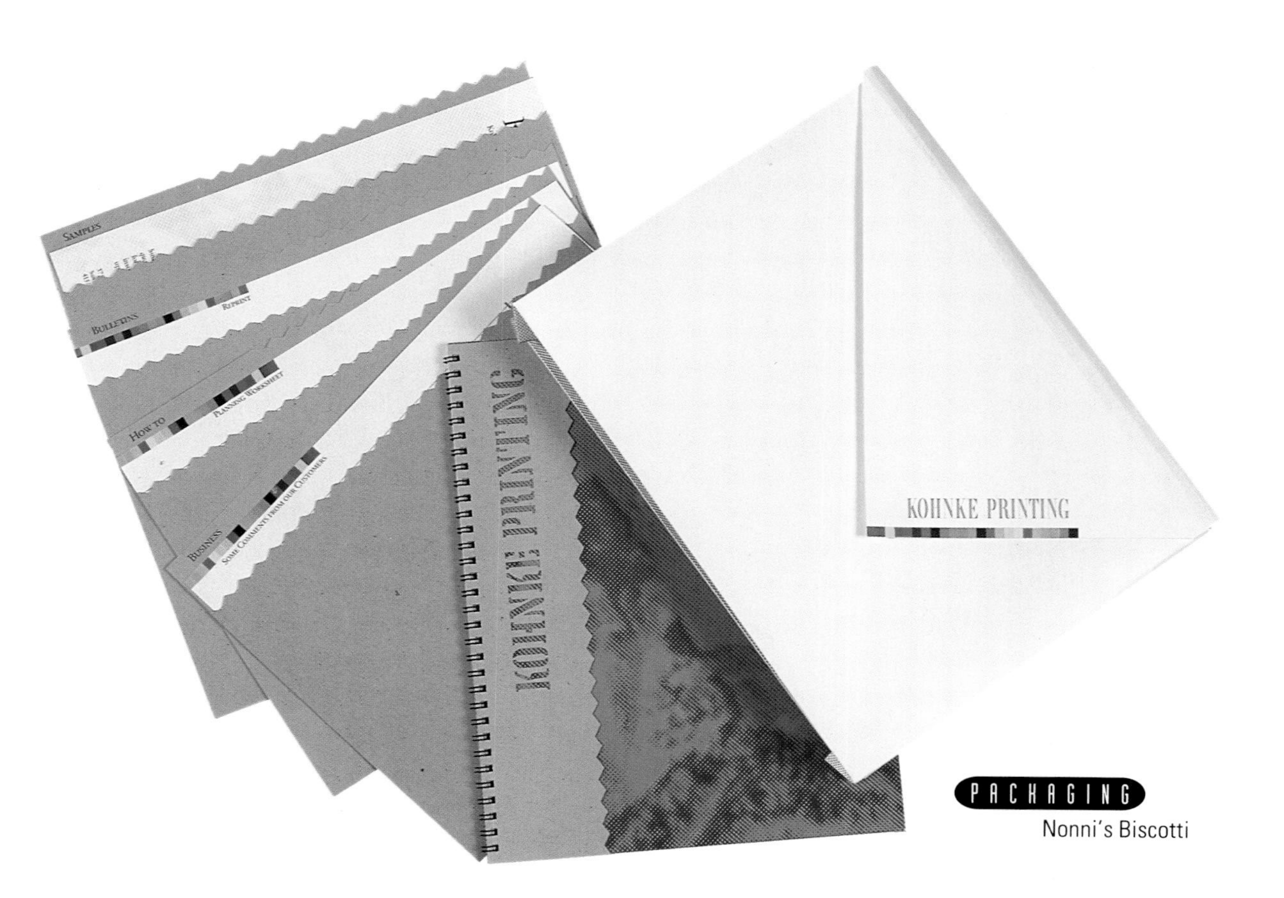

PACKAGING
Nonni's Biscotti

Cato Design Inc. Pty. Ltd.

Richmond, Victoria, Australia

Ken Cato

Kenneth Willis Cato is a member of many notable institutions, including the American Institute of Graphic Art, Type Directors Club of New York, and the Australian Type Directors Club. He is an Honorary Fellow of both the Design Institute of Australia and the Australian Marketing Institute. He has served as a keynote speaker at design seminars, forums, television, and radio programs in Europe, the United States, South America, and Asia. The work of Cato Design has been shown in many exhibitions and has won awards throughout the world. It has appeared in international publications such as *Idea* (Japan), *Graphis* (Switzerland), and *Graphis Logo 1* (USA).

BOOK COVER
View from Australia, Japanese Version

Scienceworks

PROMOTION CALENDAR

Eurasia Press

Eurasia Press

LAUNCH SCULPTURES
Laminex

"Just as we direct the use of photography and illustration, designers can also use computer graphics by way of talented freelance operators. This platform has proved a good starting point for our transition to technology. As our knowledge has developed, so has the hardware and software. We are now at a point where a computer operator specialist is a guest resident in our studio. All this without ever having had to buy a Macintosh."

Ken Cato has carefully mapped a design niche into which technology fits. "We're a studio without computers, but with easy access to computer skills. As designers, we reserve the right to answer a brief in the most appropriate way. We don't wish to be obliged to use a computer purely to cover the lease payments.

"Determining the advantages of computers in graphics depends on whether one looks within the studio or at the way industry as a whole is coping with technology. We have not forgotten that the human hand is a wonderful implement for tearing a piece of paper, scribbling with a soft crayon, splattering ink from a nib.

"Computer capability and versatility do have their price to pay. Equipment cost is not insignificant. The further into the finished art process one goes, the greater the need for more powerful computing capacity, storage, and sophisticated output equipment. For any design studio, this is a financial barrier.

"Another disadvantage is the blurring of the edges of professional distinctions. 'Designer,' 'finished artist,' 'photo-retoucher,' and 'typesetter' were once well-defined, but now they increasingly overlap. There is the expectation that one designer should perform all these crafts. Yet, the cost to employ people and supply computers is prohibitive. Design budgets have not increased at the same rate as cost of the computers.

"I'm sure that, in time, computer technology will open up interesting possibilities in the function of a design studio. But I'm not entirely convinced that the creative area will be one of those possibilities. Most certainly, we wish to reserve the right to make that decision."

MAGAZINE COVER
Edge, No. 3

WINE GIFT BOXES
Cato Design
Overseas Offices

SCULPTURE
Melbourne Olympic Bid

INVITATION
Melbourne Olympic Bid

CARRY BAGS
C'est La Vie

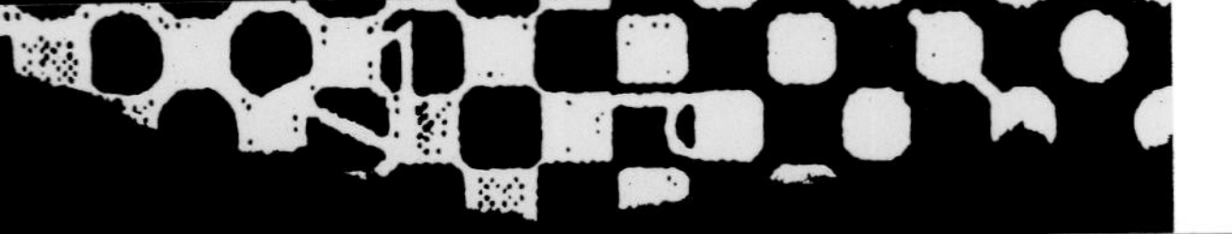

Discovery Networks Creative Services

Bethesda, Maryland, USA

Gil Cowley

Gil Cowley is a graduate of The Art Academy of Cincinnati and The Cleveland Art Institute. He was formerly art director for WCBS-TV in New York and is a founding board member and past president of The Broadcast Designers' Association. He has earned recognition from the New York and New Jersey Art Directors Clubs, The National Academy of Television Arts and Sciences, from which he earned a New York Emmy, The Broadcast Designers' Association, The New York State Broadcasters Association, The Cable Marketing Association, and The Writers Guild of America. Currently, he is responsible for the marketing ventures, associated business, and future product development of both The Discovery Channel and The Learning Channel.

It's Your World/Reach It

PROMOTIONAL KIT
The New Learning Channel

To Read

Discovery

Discovery

CLOCK
Discovery

WINE BOTTLES
Kab'ər•na'

Gil Cowley calls the complex graphic styles of The Discovery and Learning Channels a "montage." "Everything we do is so visual and our mission is so diverse, we can't explain it in one image. Our programs on The Discovery Channel, for instance, are composed of several genres — nature, human adventure, history, the environment, science and technology, education — one image cannot fit them all. To depict nature, we might use the image of an Alaskan bear. For human adventure, an ice climber. We use computers to place images together in an incongruous and intriguing manner, resulting in exciting presentations that would invite viewers, affilliates, and advertisers to our programming. Textures are also important. They introduce more colors and give something for the photos to work against. Color creates dimension, and texture personalizes it for The Discovery Channel."

Almost 1,500 jobs a year originate from Cowley's department. "Our print, video, and exhibit design are 100% computer-generated. Because of our in-house equipment, we haven't sent anything out to be typeset in years. We use computers for layout, precision, and quick changes — and we're always changing copy up to the last minute.

Discovery For Kids

Art Center College of Design
Library
1700 Lida Street
Pasadena, Calif. 91103

"In this business, computers are extremely cost-effective. Our systems have paid incalculable benefits, and we're still learning more about them. For example, we have used computers to translate video paintbox images to print by using a high-resolution paint system. It enables us, as an example, to use a video image for the video packaging without redrawing the entire concept."

Discovery projects offer dynamic examples of the range of design possible via chips, mice, and sophisticated hardware. "More than anything, I would like to stress that computers have unquestionably helped us do our jobs better. Technology's becoming transparent to the design process. We don't want to be computer gurus, we want to be designers — but designers with compatible software skills."

BROCHURE
WHY?

Get Real

T-SHIRT
Shark Week '90

BUTTONS
The Learning Channel

Earl Gee Design

San Francisco, California, USA

Earl Gee and Fani Chung

Earl Gee established his communication design firm in 1990, providing corporate identity programs, marketing and sales collateral, annual reports, product packaging, and environmental design. His clients include high-technology, medical, publishing, financial, and arts organizations. He received his degree from Art Center College of Design in California. Fani Chung, his partner, received her education at the University of Washington and earned an MFA at Yale. The firm's work has won awards from publications such as *Graphis, Communication Arts,* and *Print;* organizations including the AIGA, American Center for Design, and Type Directors Club; and is represented in the permanent collection of the Library of Congress.

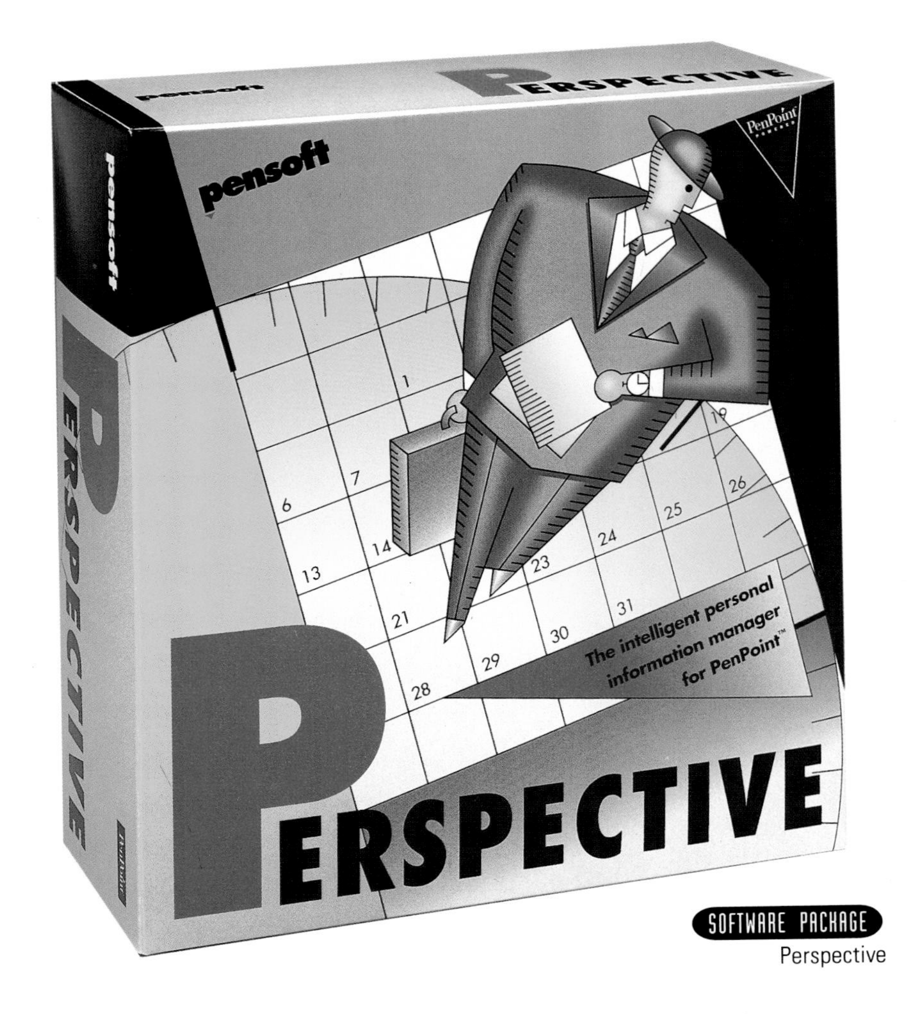

SOFTWARE PACKAGE
Perspective

Chronicle Books

ANNOUNCEMENT POSTER
Implosion Gallery

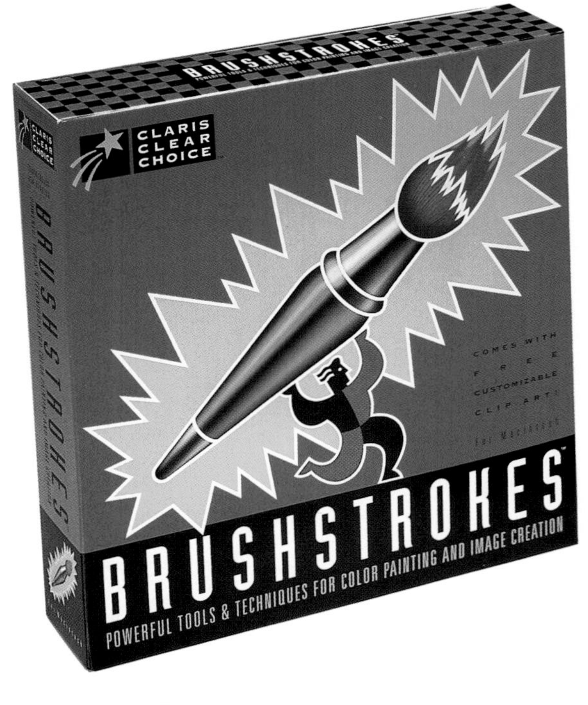

SOFTWARE PACKAGING
BrushStrokes, Retrieve It!

POSTER

Eames Lecture: "A Thousand Points of Departure . . . "

"As a designer," says Earl Gee, "my overall consideration regarding the computer is whether it is used to enhance communication. Does it help present the message more coherently, forcefully, or beautifully? Is it appropriate for the task? The answer is an emphatic 'yes' when the computer is used to its fullest potential. But the computer does design a disservice if it fails to make a message clear, does not communicate effectively, or creates images with little aesthetic value. It's the responsibility of the user to harness the power of the computer.

"As 1983 graduates, Fani and I were members of the last design school classes without computer training. We learned classic hand and eye training, drawing and hand lettering, and worked with ruling pens and brushes. But we feel we've been successful in combining an 'old school' aesthetic and attention to craft while embracing the future. We're basically self-taught on the computer. Fortunately, the technology isn't difficult to learn.

"Just as 'matte black high-tech' in product design and 'modernism' in architecture have run their course, it is actually possible for something to be too perfect. One of the effects computers cannot achieve (as of yet) is the human touch or rough look that I sometimes see missing in today's work. I don't mind a technological look as long as it has some human element, whether it's conveyed through humor or by speaking directly to the viewer, since all this technology is for the use and enjoyment of *people,* isn't it?

"We often provide our clients with electronic files for final production, allowing for easy manipulation when their products need to be localized for international markets. Our half-scale comps are done by hand, as we have found that what concerns the client most at this stage is our ideas rather than our execution.

"The computer does not act as a filtering device, the way your mind does; it can show 10,000 ways how *not* to do something as well as 10,000 ways how to do it." It's up to you, asserts Gee, to figure out which is which.

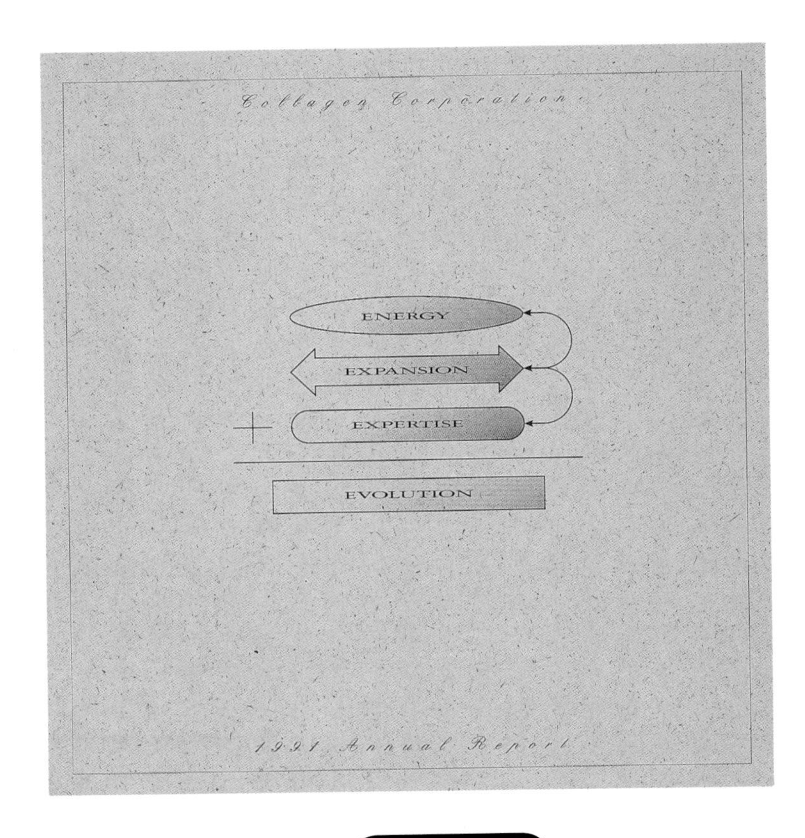

ANNUAL REPORT

Energy + Expansion + Expertise = Evolution

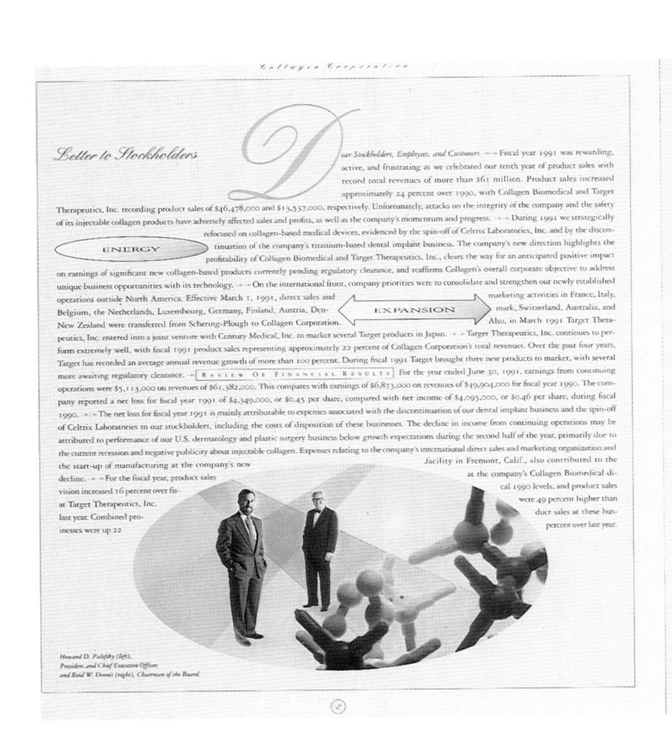

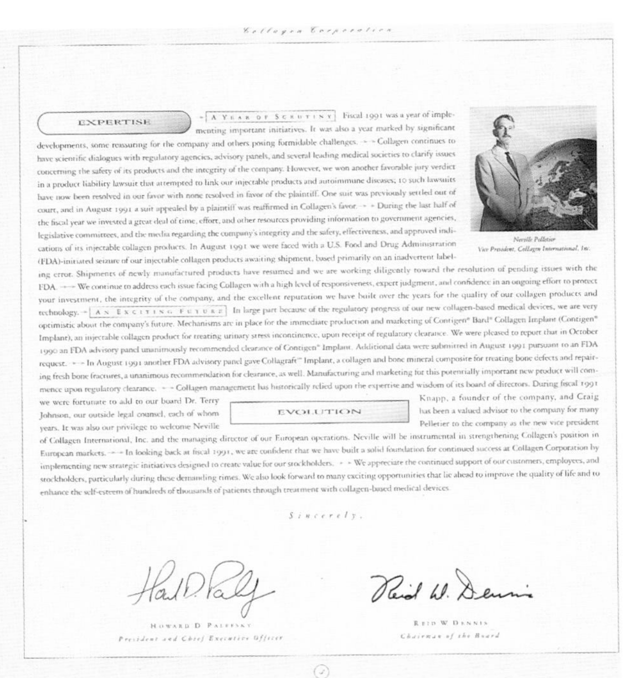

The Standard

TRADE AD

Working Asset

TRADE AD

Network Support

Evenson Design Group

Culver City, California, USA

Stan Evenson

In 1976, Stan Evenson opened a studio in California specializing in advertising and marketing programs. With a current staff of seven full-timers and a regular crew of freelance designers, Evenson Design Group has received recognition from the American Institute of Graphic Arts and the Art Directors Club of Los Angeles, among others. Evenson's works are featured in the permanent collection of the Library of Congress, and he is currently president of L.A's American Institute of Graphic Arts.

Capitol - MVP

LOGO
Radio Gabby

STATIONERY
Radio Gabby

LOGO
Private Exercise

LOGO
BeBe & CeCe Winans

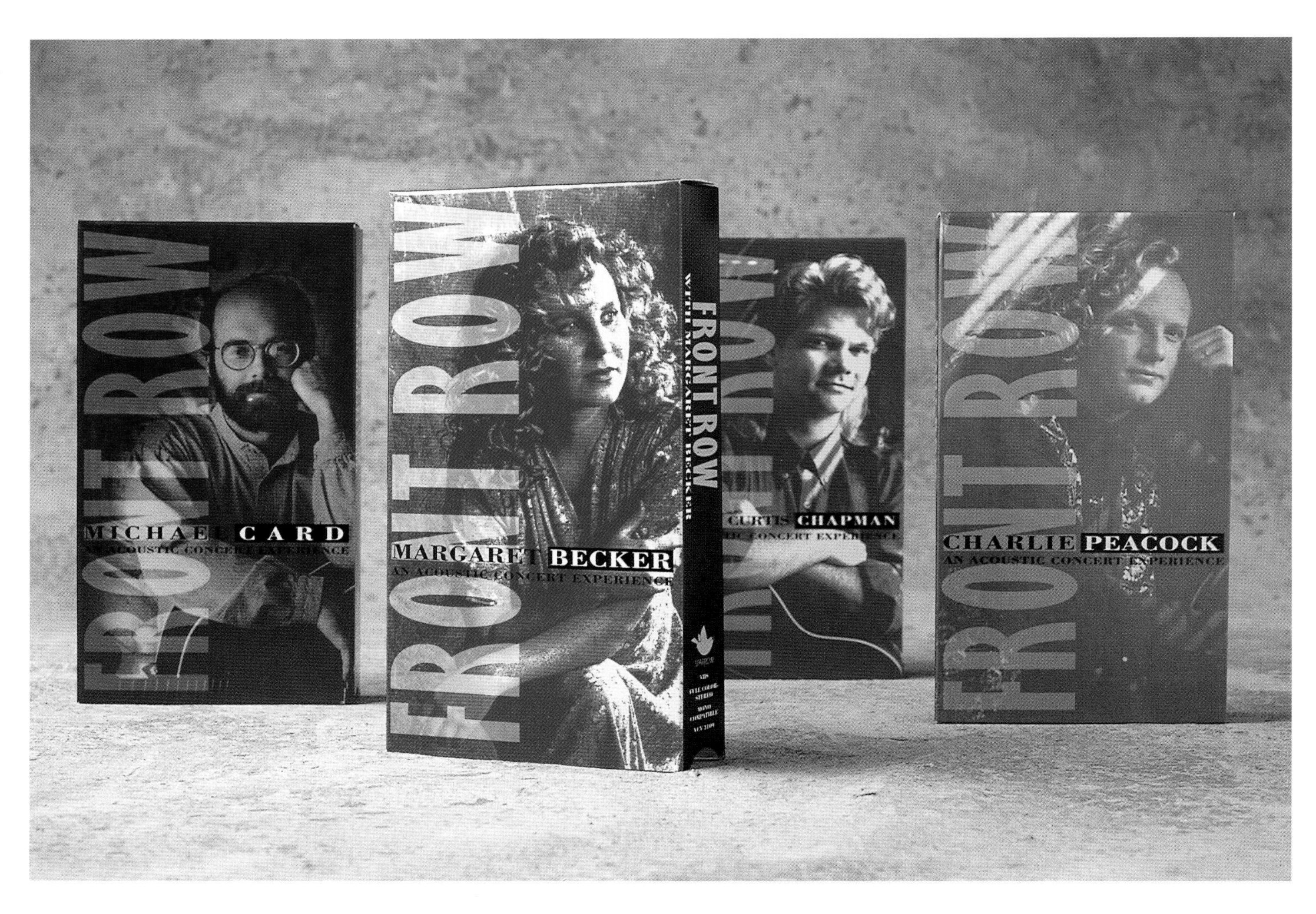

PACKAGING
Front Row Series

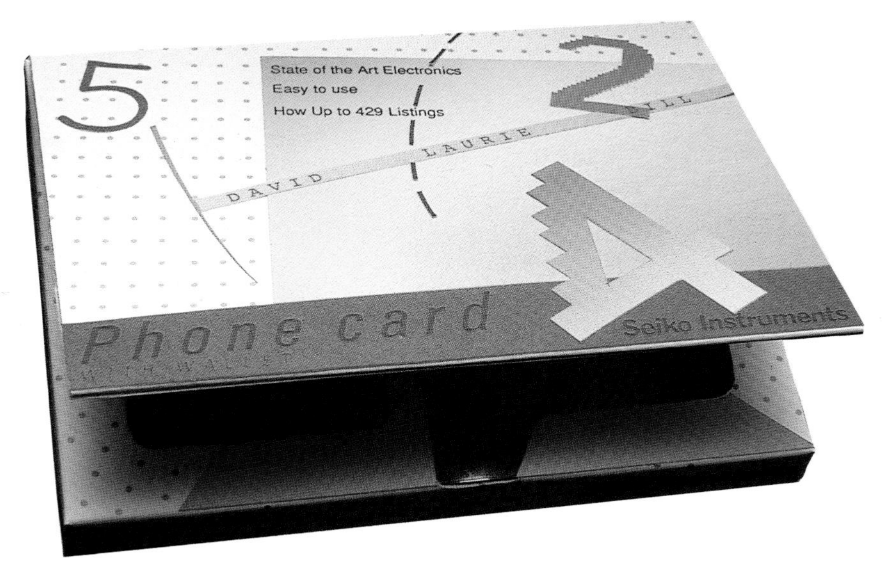

PACKAGING
Seiko Phone Card

"I don't use the computer myself," says Stan Evenson, owner of southern California's Evenson Design Group, "but I try to keep up with technology. I feel my time is best spent as the creative director and main client contact. If I were to take time to learn the computer, who's going to manage the company, bring in the business, and market our services?"

With numerous commitments outside the studio, Evenson strives for balance in his life. He has to budget his time to achieve it, and there aren't any hours left for lengthy computer training sessions. "The role of the designer is changing. As typesetters have lost out to linotronic, so designers have become typesetters, then they become integrated with color separators. I'm aware of these trends, and you have to stay in that circle or be left out in the cold." He invests in a staff with the skills necessary to use computer functions he considers critical to his business. I'm shocked that designers still exist who don't work on computers — but I'm not at all surprised that there are principals who don't.

"Clients as well as designers are all caught up in technology now. Competition is one reason we got involved — if another studio can offer more variations and color, we don't want to lose our clients to them.

AIGA/LA Freedom of Expression

"In the future, we'll have to get into interactive, digital design, and virtual reality. The printed piece won't go away, but designers will have to supplement their knowledge. There's an excitement to this. I'm constantly reevaluating our services to be more productive in our office. Technology is becoming more effective for both design and business. But you could go totally broke trying to keep up. Some designers keep reinvesting their profits in equipment, but don't evaluate if it's something they need right now. As the novelty of the computer wears off, I look forward to more humanistic design.

"Computers appeal to today's visually-driven Nintendo audience. Maybe we'll eventually use a laser beam instead of a printing press. Methods will continue to change, but effects will still be appreciated."

CALL FOR ENTRIES
Prism Awards

PROMOTIONAL KIT

Squirt Force

PROMOTIONAL BOOKLET

Martha Productions Inc.

FHA Design

South Melbourne, Victoria, Australia

Richard Henderson, Trevor Fleet,

and Jeff Arnold

FHA Design was established by Trevor Flett, Richard Henderson, and Jeff Arnold in 1976. With offices in Melbourne, Sydney, and Singapore, FHA specializes in corporate identity, packaging, signage, retail, and environmental design. The company philosophy is one of a "holistic view" — the concept of the "added value" knowledge, reason, skill, experience, commitment, understanding, and vision provide, which translates into value for the client's marketing dollars. The work of the company has been represented in *Graphis, Idea, Communication Arts,* and numerous other international and Australian publications. Henderson and Flett are co-founders of the Australian Graphic Design Association.

Biomolecular Research Institute

LOGO
Greenmill Dance Project

POSTER
Greenmill Dance Project

STATIONERY
Laine Furnishings

BROCHURE
Ansett Technologies

LOGO
Top of the Bay

CLOTHING APPLICATION
Top of the Bay

"Harnessing technology to simplify processes and reduce waste while achieving a desirable product — this is our approach to computers," says Richard Henderson, one of three partners and a staff of 13 that compose FHA Design. "This reflects our business development from ruling pen to rotring, letraset to omnicron, hot metal to photo typesetting. The computer offers us the opportunity to produce all these from one source — efficiently, effectively, and economically. Most importantly, it allows us to control the final result — to remove the factor of chance."

To Henderson, computer-generated design means "beguiling and exquisitely delicate imagery can be achieved with cool precision. Our designers, however, do not have terminals at their desks. Ideas are generated through inquiry and evolution using paper and pencil. Computers cannot feel the exhiliration of the creative process — but they can certainly empower the resolution. It is our computer personnel who convert the rough layouts of our designers into artwork.

"On a project-by-project basis, we fill gaps left by the elimination of middle management. We operate as a resource to our clients by going into their offices and helping them input design strategies and understand how the job will be done cost-effectively. We even use the Mac to put projects on disk with instructions, which clients can use to produce documents like manuals internally.

MENU & MATCHES
Level One

STOREFRONT
Australia on Collins

"A decade ago, we embraced technology by finding a designer who had 'caught the bug' and could interpret computer potential from a designer's viewpoint. From this fragile beginning, we learned even more by attracting people who enjoyed the concept of combining technology with creativity. The ongoing challenge is to find people who can interface with the studio's day-to-day operations and also communicate, both verbally and visually; we don't want computer people who drift into semi-symbiotic states, isolated from normal interaction, crazed with system overload and software hallucinations."

At FHA, computer literacy is not a prerequisite for design superiority. "After all, you don't have to understand the technological workings of a BMW motor car to be able to achieve optimum performance. But you do have to be a good driver."

LOGO
Australia on Collins

Level One

Typo Mac

Kinetik Communication Graphics, Inc.

Washington, D.C., USA

Jeffrey Fabian and Samuel Shelton

Jeffrey Fabian and Samuel Shelton, both graduates of Virginia Commonwealth University, are partners in Washington, D.C.'s Kinetik Communication Graphics, which was founded in 1988. Among their awards in print design is recognition from the American Institute of Graphic Arts, The Art Directors Club of Metropolitan Washington, American Center for Design, Type Directors Club, and *Print* magazine. Their work can be seen in many publications, including *Communication Arts.*

BOOK
Herald Square

A Votre Santé

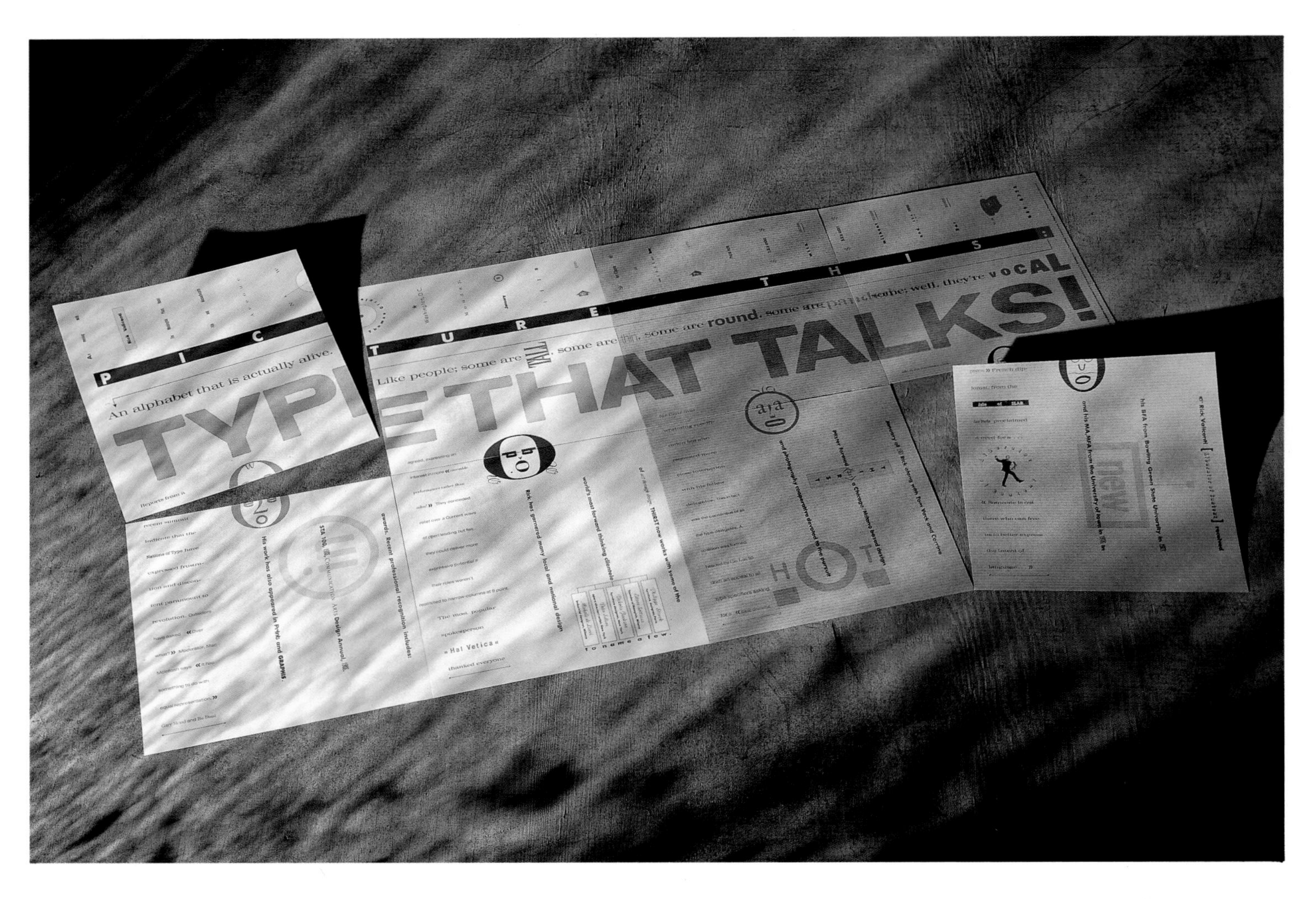

LECTURE INVITATION
Type That Talks

PROMOTION
Jingle Java

SELF PROMOTION
Leap Day

Jeff Fabian admits to mixed feelings about the impact of computers on design. "It opened up doors to complex solutions and increased the range of possibilities. On the other hand, we don't want to be forced to be color separators, strippers, or typesetters, either."

Unlike some of his industry counterparts, Fabian is not compelled to learn all the latest technology. In fact, sometimes he doesn't use the computer at all. "We actually have a mandate here to occasionally bypass the computer entirely. This can happen after we complete a large, computer-intensive project, partially because we're simply tired of sitting in front of a screen. A computer does some things so easily, it can become a crutch, and you have to step back in order to get something interesting again. With a fresh perspective, we can see the computer is not automatically the most appropriate method for a project.

Kids Count

It's the hands-on aspect of design that Fabian favors — techniques learned in college at a time when the Mac hadn't even been invented. "I think we were taught more traditional problem-solving without the computer. Computers, in some ways, have renewed interest in and regard for traditional processes, the way the industrial revolution was the impetus for the arts and crafts movement. Technology doesn't intimidate us, but the computer often feels more limiting than sketching.

"To meet the requirements of some clients and remain compatible with particular programs, we've learned a lot about technology. Clients such as National Geographic are entirely electronic. But it's a transitional period for the industry, so we're reluctant to make predictions for the next decade. We're not resisting technology, but we're not aggressively embracing it, either. We're interested in new software and attend workshops to learn more. It's a challenge to ensure we don't get overwhelmed by trying to keep up, however."

A World of Animals

PACKAGING
Wonders of Learning
CD ROM

COMPACT DISC
Interlochen Center
for the Arts

KROG

Ljubljana, Slovenia

Edi Berk

Edi Berk graduated from Ljubljana Universiti's Faculty of Architecture. In 1982, he founded Studio KROG, and entered a partnership in 1984 with school colleague, architect, and interior designer Andrej Mlakar. Berk has displayed his work in exhibits throughout Eastern and Western Europe, the U.S., Canada, Mexico, Israel, and Japan. Berk's work has been published in numerous magazines and books, such as *Designers Self-Image* and *Graphis Poster 92*. One of his most well-known efforts was designing a series of advertising campaigns promoting the positive image of emerging democratic youth work programs for the former Liberal Party of Slovenia, ZSMS.

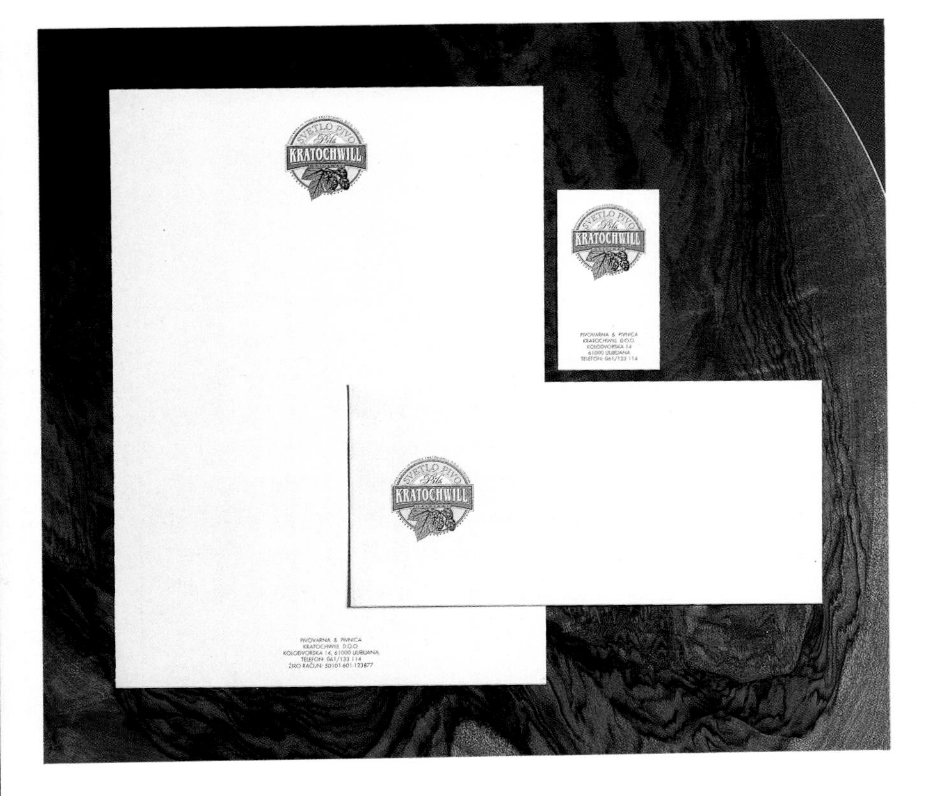

STATIONERY

Kratochwill Brewery

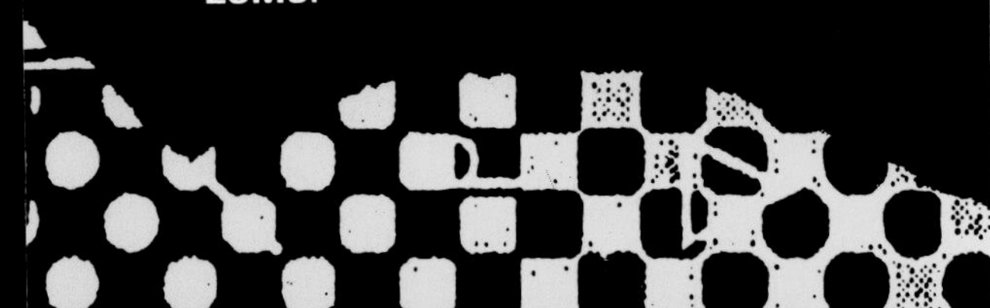

BROCHURE

Vili Ravnjak: Tugomer

PROZAIČNA VIRTUOZNOST

Na prvi pogled je tale pozabljena komedija izpred 300 let doživela zasluženo usodo. Ponuja nekaj odsluženih stereotipov, ki niso več smešni niti načrtovalcem pouka književnosti, zapovrh pa so še silno razvlečeni; en ljubimec ne more do svoje izbranke, ker je ta v krempljih zlobnih skrbnikov; drugi je preveč navdušen nad spogledovanjem (in še čim več), da bi se dal speljati v zakonski jarem, a ga njegova dama nazadnje s preizkušenim shakespearjevskim trikom (preobleko oz. zamenjavo spola) le ujame; lokav koristolovec si najde bogato in neumno nevesto, a je na koncu le ugnan v kozji rog; naslovna junakinja bi z malo domišljije lahko bila za vzor legendarnemu Goethejevemu Wertherju. Ti štirje in še drugi dovolj znani motivi so vsi zbasani v "Nedolžni ljubici" – gre za še zavidanja vreden muzejski tekst... Ampak – se iz vsega tega na sodobnem odru da narediti kaj, kar bi imelo še kakšno drugo kot le muzejsko vrednost?

Nekoliko pozornejše branje pa preseneti: pod sila tanko površino odnosov, kakršne poznamo iz sentimentalnih romanov, se skriva precej bolj realistična plast – vsi ljubezenski pari so namreč socialno povsem nesporni. Priljubljena komedija iz časa nastanka "Nedolžne ljubice" se imenuje "Marriage à la mode"... Tudi v "Nedolžni ljubici" se poročajo med seboj junaki, ki so si ne samo simpatični, ampak tudi in predvsem primerni drug za drugega. Odkritje v zvezi z "Nedolžno ljubico" je, da nimamo opravka z usodnimi čustvi, ampak s premišljenimi nagnjenji, ki imajo podlago v družbenem ozadju celotnega besedila in tudi dobe, v kateri je nastalo. Vse t.i. ljubezenske zveze so zelo comme il faut, nobena niti najmanj ne seže čez meje dopustnega: pomembna razlika med "Nedolžno ljubico" in npr. "Pahljačo", ki jo MGL letos tudi uprizarja, je, da so v primerjavi z junaki "Pahljače" junaki "Nedolžne ljubice" izrazito normalni. Morda bi se jim dalo očitati vsakemu kakšno drobno posebnost, ampak te so prej osebna nota kot pomanjkanje inteligence, ki je pri protagonistih "Pahljače" ponekod kar prećejšnja. Prozaičnost junakov "Nedolžne ljubice" raste prav iz tega, da so nam tako blizu, da je njihovo obnašanje navsezadnje tako podobno našemu lastnemu.

TUKIDID, ARHIVAR IN FILOZOF STAROGRŠKE ZGODOVINE, JE V SPISU "PATOLOGIJA VOJNE" DEFINIRAL VOJNO KOT KINESIS (GIBANJE), KI CELOTNO GRŠTVO POŽENE IZ TEDANJEGA NAČINA ŽIVLJENJA. VOJNA POSTANE UČITELJ NASILJA, TAKIM OKOLIŠČINAM PA PRILAGODI TUDI ČUSTVA VEČINE LJUDI. GRŠKI ZGODOVINOPISEC TAKO ŽE ZELO ZGODAJ OPOZORI NA POPOLNO TRANSFORMACIJO ETIČNIH NORM IN VREDNOT, NA SPREMEMBO KODOV, KI DOLOČAJO RAZUMEVANJE, CELO NA SPREMEMBO JEZIKA, KI JO POVZROČA VOJNA. V VOJNEM ČASU SO PORUŠENI VSI POGOJI SKUPNEGA (PRI TUKIDIDU POLISNEGA) ŽIVLJENJA. TO JE OBODBJE ZMAGOSLAVJA TAKE ČLOVEŠKE NARAVE, KI DAJE PREDNOST MAŠČEVALNOSTI PRED SVETOSTJO, PRIDOBITNIŠTVU PRED ŽIVLJENJEM BREZ ZLOČINA – IN KADAR LJUDJE SNUJEJO MAŠČEVALNA DEJANJA, BREZOBZIRNO RAZDIRAJO SKUPNE ZAKONE O TAKŠNIH DEJANJIH. TA SVOJEVRSTNI TEKST JE TAKO EDEN OD PRVIH OPISOV VOJNE, KI OPOZARJA NA MNOŽIČNO ETIČNO DEGRADACIJO ŽIVLJENJA V VOJNEM ČASU. VZROK TAKEGA PONIŽANJA ČLOVEŠKE BITI PA JE V POPOLNI IGNORANCI ZAKONA, KI OMOGOČA ŽIVLJENJE V SKUPNOSTI. HISTERIJA VOJNE PORUŠI RAVNOTEŽJE BIVANJA IN VZPOSTAVI STANJE NEN-(A)-RAVNOSTI.

Ena od mnogih zgodb o neuravnoteženem, disharmoničnem času, je tudi Tugomerova zgodba, mit o mladeniču in izdajalcu. Ta mit se v Ravnjakovi drami "Tisti, ki meri žalost" razkriva kot prepoznavanje različnosti človeškega hrepenenja po ravnovesju. Histerija vojne je zajela Karantanijo, karantanski knez je zahrbtno ubit, njegova žena, Tugomerova mati, iz obupa naredi samomor, prelita kri kliče po maščevanju. Tugomer je po težavnosti odločitve podoben velikim tragedijskim junakom (Orest, Hamlet), saj mora uravnavati svojo usodo sredi neuravnoteženega sveta. Neravnovesje namreč transformira odnose med človekom in usodo, med naravo in kozmosom, med posvetnim in svetim.

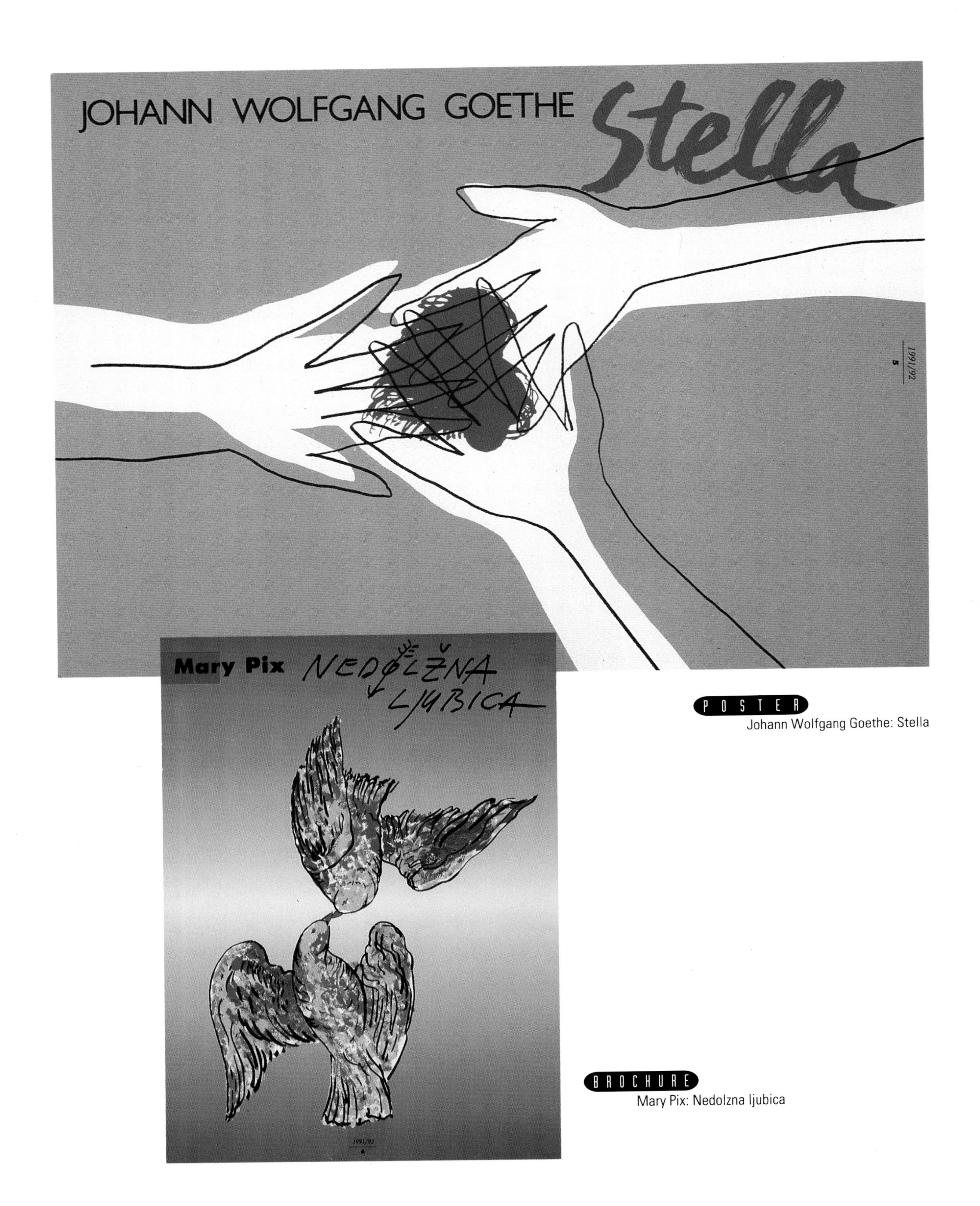

POSTER
Johann Wolfgang Goethe: Stella

BROCHURE
Mary Pix: Nedolzna ljubica

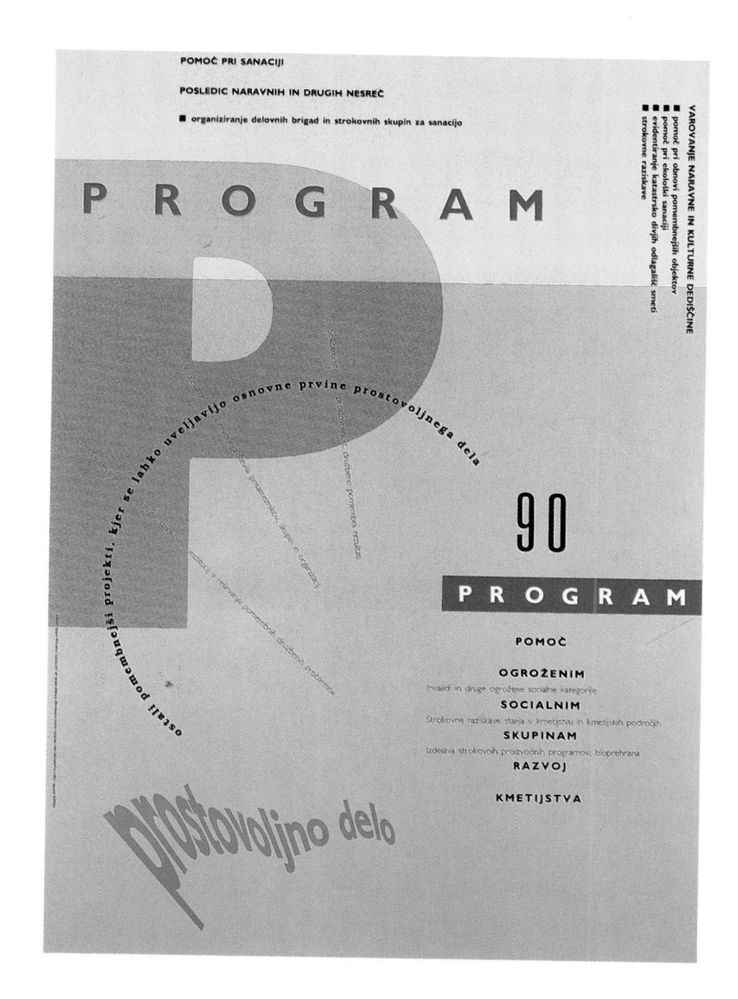

Oblike 90

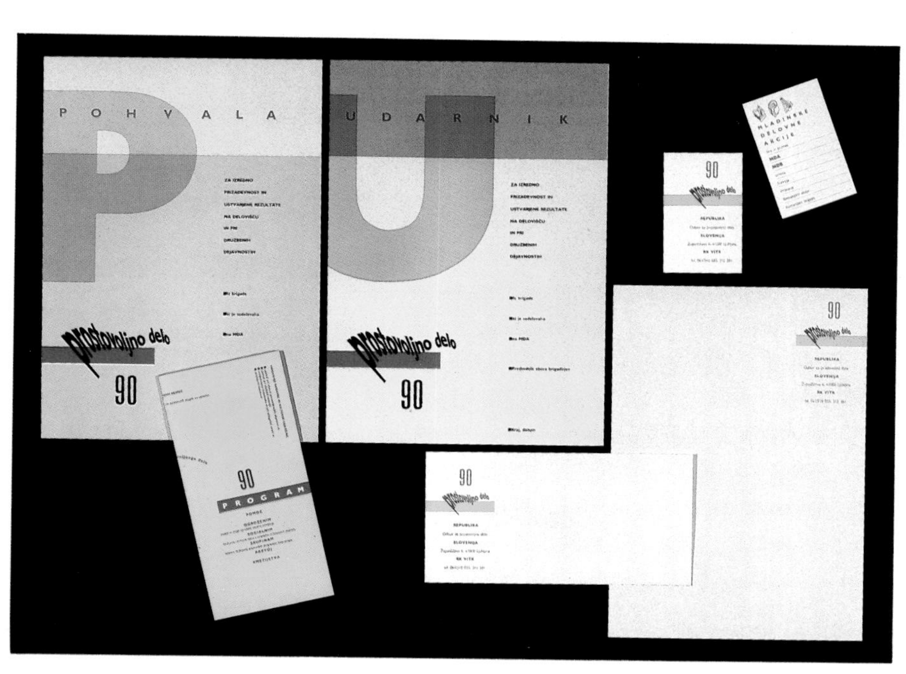

IDENTITY
Program 90

Although most of Edi Berk's work is produced on the computer, he still prefers to draw logotypes by hand. "It's easier," he says. "I feel more comfortable checking the proportions, spacing, and measurements on paper first. A screen and paper are different; on paper, a symbol is much clearer."

Berk uses computers for magazine spreads, illustrations, and headlines for posters. "You can make corrections more quickly on a computer. Design that involves a great deal of detail work — lines, curves, combining many different kinds of typography, such as designing the shares for a bank — also lends itself well to computers. I used the computer to design beer labels for a brewery. But the name of the brewery I chose to draw by hand."

BROCHURE
Ephraim Kishon: Bil je skrjanec

One of the two principals of Studio KROG, Berk does not own a computer, but uses local technical firms that sell time and services. Technology can be expensive in eastern Europe — currently, a Macintosh costs from $10,000 to $30,000. But, for Berk, it's not the money that deters him from purchasing his own equipment. "I don't have the two or three months necessary to learn the computer if I owned one. Instead, I have many friends in companies who purchase U.S. software, and I rent their technology to use as design support." He takes his sketches to an outside firm for typesetting, and the firm also lays out the print piece. "They work according to my rule," he states. The partnership works well for both parties.

Schooled in architecture, Berk graduated from the local university and entered the workforce when the climate in Slovenia had become very difficult, both politically and economically. "After 1980, each year got harder. Buildings could not be built because the economy was weak. I learned graphic design as an alternative, then found it was a field of creation that gave even more pleasure than architecture." Shortly thereafter, Berk discovered computers. Now more than 90% of his work is in computer-aided design.

BROCHURE
Luigi Pirandello: Kaj je resnica

BROCHURE

Industrial Design
Education in the World

NORWAY

Statens Håndverks-og Kunstindustriskole, Oslo,
Insitutt for Industridesign
The National College of Art and Design,
Institute of Industrial Design, Institute of Furniture
Ullevålsveien 5, 0165 Oslo, Norway
Tel. 47/2/20 12 35, after 3.00 p.m. 20 12 12 + ext. 291,
Fax. 47/2/11 14 96 or 11 31 20

The Institute's professional and educational structure aims to serve the European industrial structure, which implies the challenges of internationalization. We define our curriculum as a project-integrated educational structure. The structure is divided into two major objectives, – basic skills in 10 main subjects to form the formal profile of competence, and 14 theme based projects for development of versatile experiences. The subjects (and sub-subjects) serve the theme-based project in order to throw light on specific subjective aspects within the various professional situations that we prepare our candidates to be able to meet in their careers as professionals.

The 14 projects are defined with increasing complexity, both in the number of subjects involved and in the interaction with external players such as industries and R&D organizations. ☐ The Institute offers studies with advanced technical equipment such as Alias Studio Design on Silicon Graphics hardware and a computer-interactive ergonomics laboratory. Special emphasis is put on the ability to understand and control the mutual interplay between form, material and production processes, and to bring these basic design concepts within the frameworks of both economic and market customer oriented design development. In the fields of R&D the institute has established extensive links and professional cooperation with business schools, industries and various technical and humanistic R&D organizations. ☐ Over the last few years the institute has faced the challenge to bring about an extensive consciousness of the qualities of our *object culture* as a major comparative measurement in the fields of cultural identity and development. ☐ Through NCAD we foresee the launching of a PhD-program within 3-4 years. The annual number of student entries is limited to 12. The total number of students is 60. ☐ The professional staff including professors, senior scientific lecturers, regular lecturers and administration is for the time being 16. In addition the Institute offers external tutors both as project managers and as subject lecturers. Each year of the 4,5 year study includes a study tour/visit within Europe according to the semesterial theme. IFID is located in a separate renewed building close to the main building, and offers the students 1400 m^2 of sophisticated laboratories, exhibition area, tutorial/lecturing rooms, individual workspaces, student lobby and workshops. ☐

66

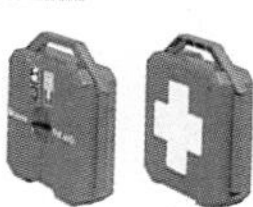

COMPLETE MEDICAL EMERGENCY KIT.
DIPLOMA 1989

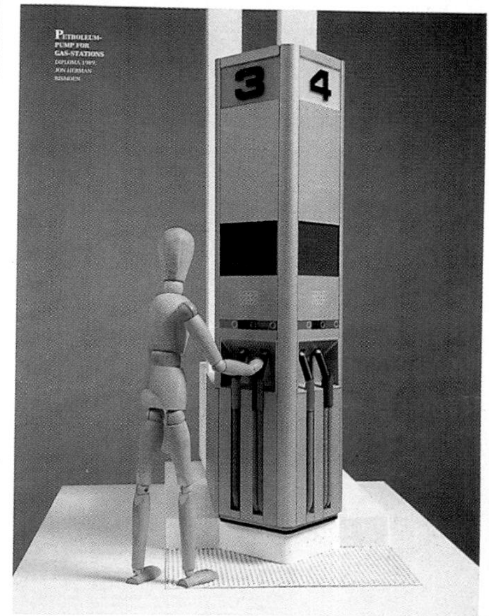

PETROLEUM-PUMP FOR GAS-STATIONS
DIPLOMA 1989

problem and application of the related
FORMING
criteria of industrial design
A DESIGNER'S
The ability to use and apply notions of
PERSONALITY
other scientific disciplines.

The development of craft abilities in the
building of models with emphasis on the
whole presentation of the proposal
including graphic documentation.

29

- methods of self-knowledge and the development of creative work

Theoretical subjects
- orientated to the general coherence of the development of art and culture
- history of fine art
- history of spiritual and material culture
- aesthetics

History of design
- development of design from its "prehistorical" period up to the present time with a prognostic overlap into the future
- analysis of reasons for the formation of the new profession of designer and the gradual change of its character
- creation of individual design personalities, national schools and design styles

Theory and methods of design
- design as a means of communication
- form as a bearer of expression and meaning
- design as a component of ecology
- philosophical aspects of the design creation
- the specific methods of creation of design in various fields of its operation (graphic product and industrial design)
- the basic means of the formation of design

CARRIAGE FOR DISABLED

VIDEO-CAMERA
5TH YEAR

Modern Dog

Seattle, Washington, USA

Robynne Raye, Michael Strassburger, and Vittorio Costarella

Modern Dog was co-founded in 1987 by Western Washington University graduates Robynne Raye and Michael Strassburger to "produce offbeat, original design inspired by our work as painters and musicians." Vittorio Costarella joined the firm in 1991. With a client list that includes K2 Snowboards and Warner Bros. Records, the firm has been honored with a silver medal from the New York Art Directors Club and awards of merit from *HOW*, Washington Trademark Design, Type Directors Club, and AIGA. *Print's* Regional Design Annual has featured Modern Dog for three consecutive years.

STAFF JACKET
One Reel

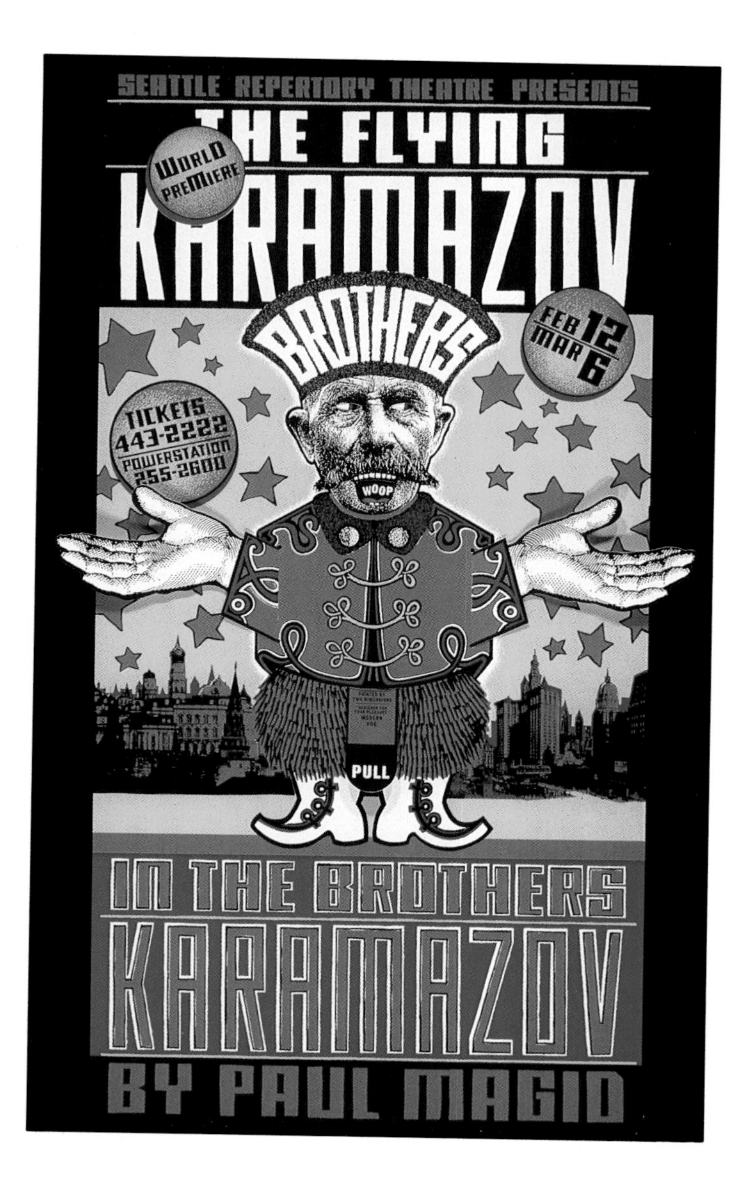

POSTER
The Flying Karamazov Brothers

LEATHER PATCH
Red Eraser

BROCHURE
K2 Wakeboard

UMBRELLA
Bumbershoot

"The prevailing attitude is, why do it by hand when you can do it on computer?" claims Robynne Raye, one Modern Dog Design principal. "Our attitude is, why do it on computer when you can do it by hand?"

Regardless of their attitude, every design from Modern Dog's studio has been "altered, modified, shrunk, enlarged, distorted, or turned inside out" by the computer. But "none have been born inside a computer, or even reached puberty there," says Raye. "They're conceived on a drafting table, and enter the computer as the final stop on the way out the door. Much of design has become homogenized by technology. We've made a conscious effort to keep our hand-crafted look while incorporating computers in our work."

Asserts co-founder Michael Strassburger, "We will never have a computer-design look, no matter how much work we do on the computer. Designers develop new styles on the computer as a result of what the computer does naturally. It comes easily, and I believe everybody goes through this stage when learning to design with technology. But some designers seem to not grow out of this phase. The solution should not be an exercise in a designer's learning curve, but the best solution possible, regardless of the designer's technical skills."

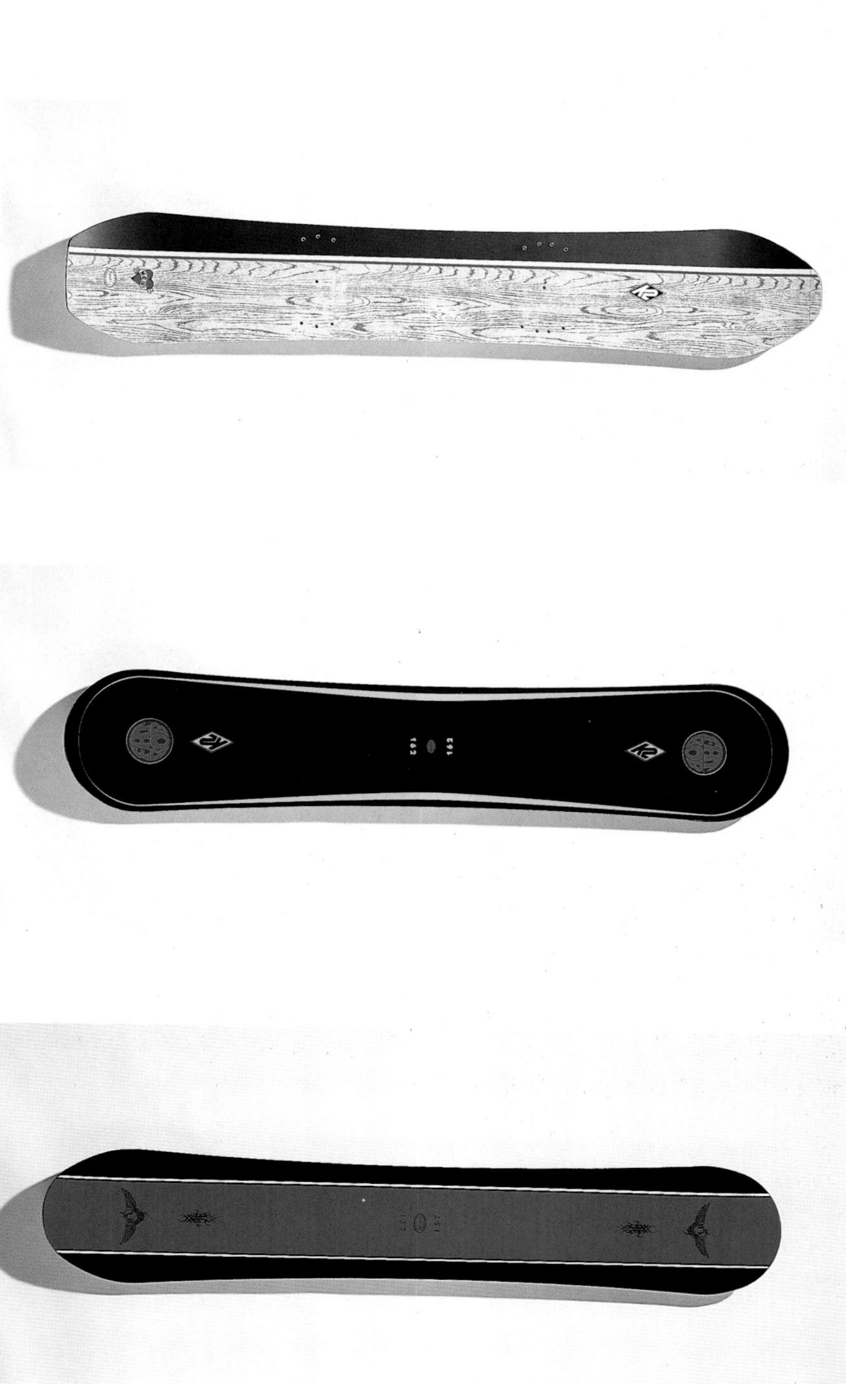

K2 Snowboards

LIPS TOGETHER,
Teeth Apart
by Terrence McNally
Seattle Repertory Theatre • Jan. 6 - 30 • Tickets 443.2222 PowerStation 255.2600
Poster by Modern Dog. Printing by Two Dimensions with water-based inks on recycled paper.

POSTER
Lips Together, Teeth Apart

"It's been frustrating and exciting," says Vittorio Costarella, the third arm of Modern Dog. "I think, overall, our design has improved. We experiment more with color and type, but we are not masters of the computers."

Raye explains, "Our design generally relies on illustration. I was afraid computers would take away that edge. So we hesitated until we started losing jobs to studios with computers. Incorporating computers into our studio is a means of survival.

"Last year, no one here knew beans about a computer. One year later, we've taught ourselves what we need to know. We continue to learn as fast as we can."

ADVERTISEMENT
Billboard Magazine

Neville Brody Studio

London, England

Neville Brody

Neville Brody studied graphic design at the Hornsey College of Art and the London College of Printing. His early work was in record sleeve design at companies such as Stiff and Fetish Records, then as art director of the magazine *The Face.* There he transformed magazine design worldwide, with his type approach widely copied. Brody now runs his own studio, and joined FontShop, a network of computer typeface supply sources, in 1990. Among his recent projects, Brody redesigned the station identity for ORF, the Austrian national broadcasting system. Much of Brody's work is from Japanese corporate, fashion, music, and publishing companies. In 1989, a Brody exhibition in Germany attracted over 60,000 visitors and, in 1990, it toured Japan.

Fuse 1

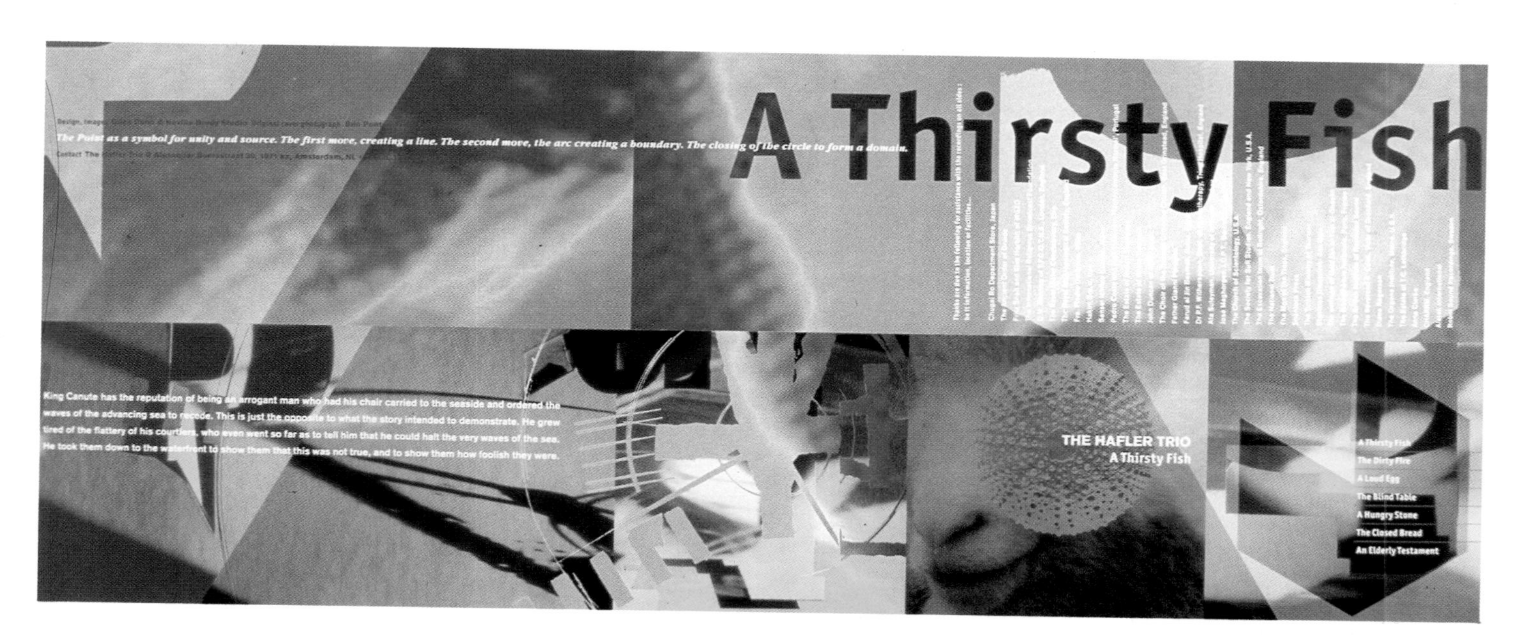

PROMOTIONAL POSTER
The Hafler Trio/A Thirsty Fish

PROMOTIONAL POSTER
Digitalogue

PROMOTIONAL POSTER
Saiten Klänge

PROMOTIONAL POSTER
World Street Music Festival

PROMOTIONAL POSTER
Gespannt auf . . . /Wolfgang Leonhard

"My approach to computers is like painting — use them expressively, not as a mathematical program," explains Neville Brody. "You shouldn't be restricted by one program, but freely move between them. Understand as much as possible, because if you don't, the computer will control you. In painting, you learn about color; in technology, if you don't learn the computer options, default values will be chosen for you in typeface or grid or page size. You have to learn enough to effectively alter all those elements.

"The computer allows you to do two things: to produce something in a logical, ordered fashion, and to process things. Unfortunately, the strongest processes on the machine are graphic tricks, like stretching type, for instance. As it becomes easier to do, everyone does it. I hate when I see design that's made up only of putting type on a circle — it's just an easy trick. People put type sideways just because you can. The radical approach is not to use computer tricks.

"Many people assume computers will alter the way you work and think. The reality is, in terms of controlling the creative aspect, the computer has made little difference. It saves time, but it causes as much grief when things go wrong. It's easy to produce 50 logos rather than just five, but the *idea* for 50 would not be any better than the idea for five."

Brody's studio is completely computer-based. "Everyone who works here is computer-savvy and experienced in other areas of hand craft, like painting or life-drawing from models. Hand crafts offer you a sense of seeing. Drawing frees one from grids and structures, and that experience allows you to use computers in a more organic way. The computer can be rigid and geometric; unless you've had the experience of using your eyes and hands in a different way, you won't challenge the machine."

Where is technology heading? "I don't know. Maybe the next step is throwing the computer out of the window and going back to using mud and clay, something more primitive and unsophisticated. I think there may be a strong tendency back towards something much more humanistic and away from obviously computer design; music, for instance, is going back to acoustic instruments. In all, not even the solution is as important as the creative process. The things we work on have to be *despite* the technology, not *because* of it."

PROMOTIONAL POSTER
Gioblitz

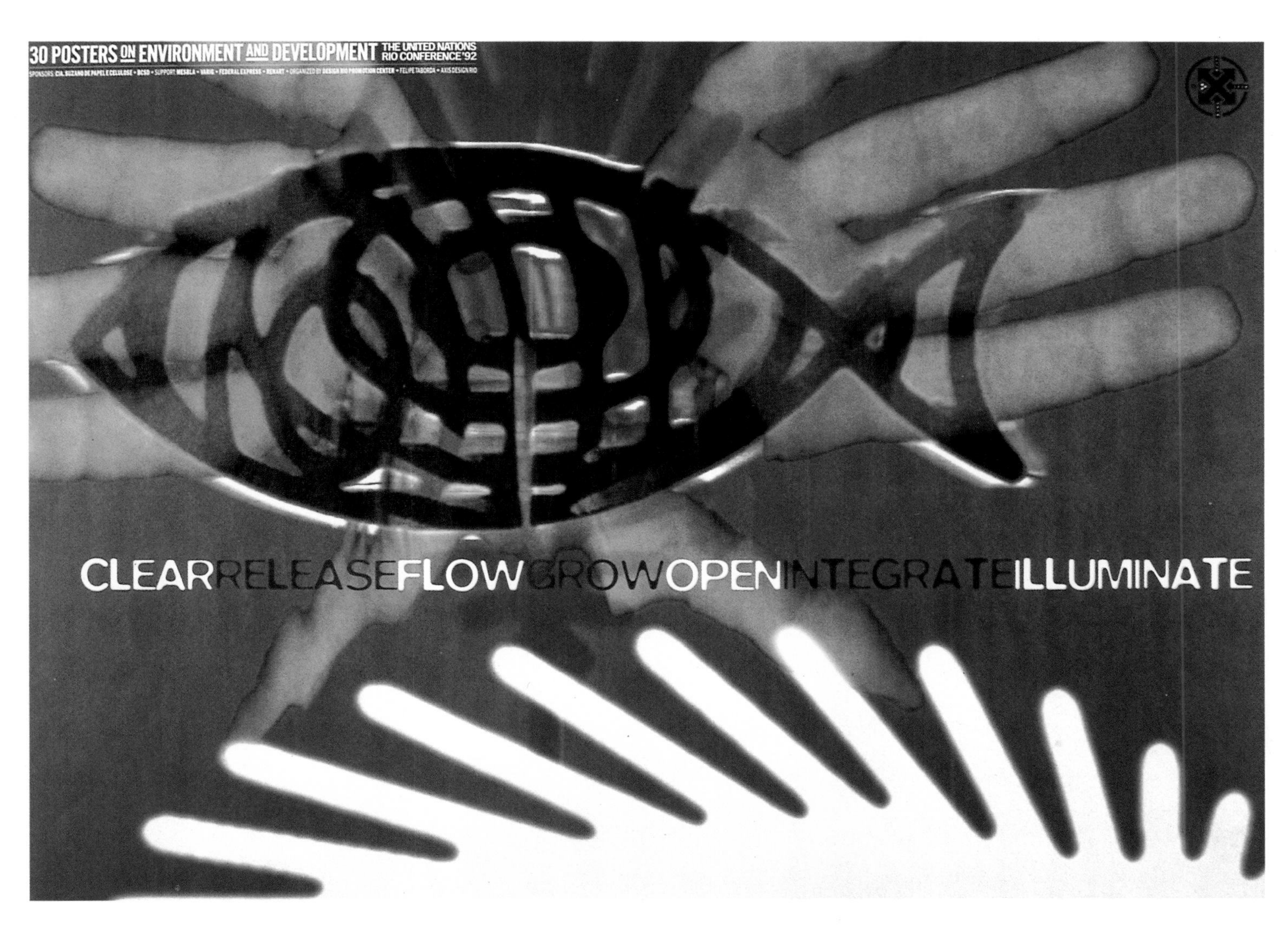

PROMOTIONAL POSTER

30 Posters on Environment and Development, The United Nations Rio Conference '92

PROMOTIONAL POSTER

GAM

Pat Taylor, Inc.

Washington, D.C., USA

Pat Taylor

Oi Veerasarn

Pat Taylor is Pat Taylor Inc., a one-man corporation specializing in logotypes and magazine design and production. Established in 1969 in Appleton, Wisconsin, Taylor moved to Washington, D.C. in 1971 to concentrate on magazines and other printed material. Taylor has received awards in graphic design from numerous Art Directors Clubs, as well as the Typographers International Association, Society of Publication Designers, National Composition Association, The Ozzie Awards, AIGA50, and Washington Trademark Design Awards. His work has been published in Japan, Mexico, and the United States. Taylor has lectured on design at the Smithsonian Institution and at various colleges and universities.

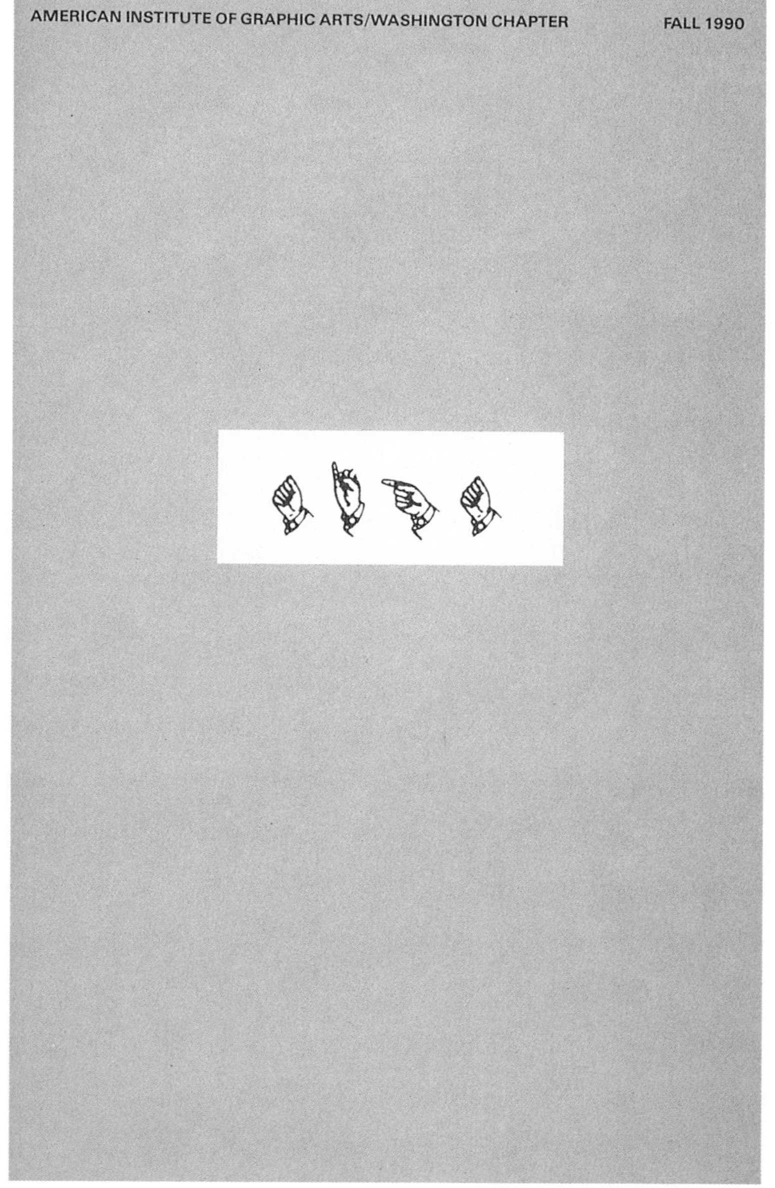

QUARTERLY JOURNAL
AIGA, Fall 1990

AIGA, Winter 1991

QUARTERLY JOURNAL
AIGA, Spring 1990

AMERICAN INSTITUTE OF GRAPHIC ARTS/WASHINGTON CHAPTER SUMMER 1990

QUARTERLY JOURNAL
AIGA, Summer 1990

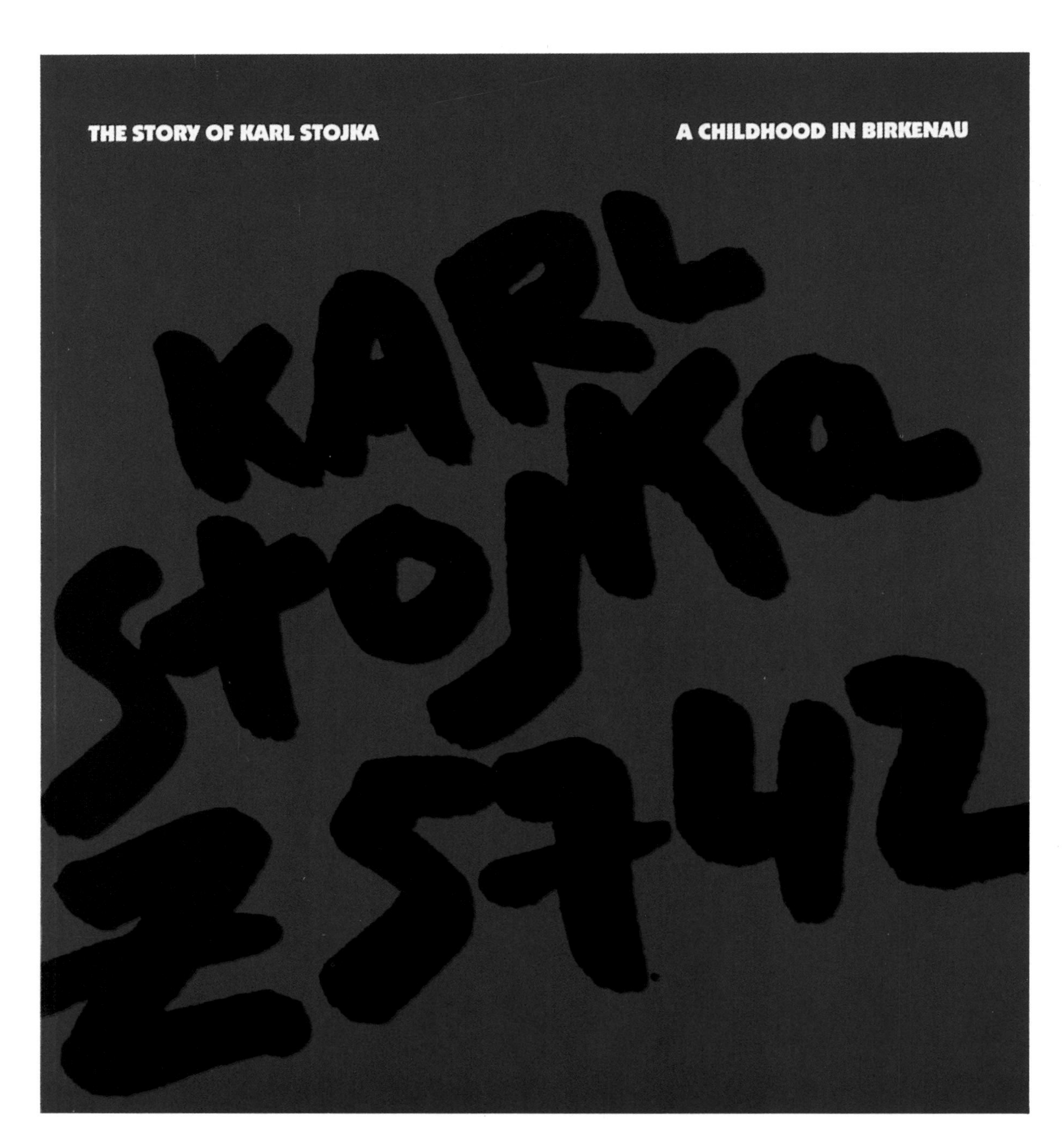

CATALOG
The Story of Karl Stojka

LOGO
Wisconsin Star Publishers

Frank Evans Art Supplies

"I call myself an artist," says Pat Taylor, principal of Washington, D.C.'s Pat Taylor Inc., "so I'm committed to producing artwork with personality, not rubber-stamped machine products. By definition, the artist dwells in the world of the pure and the aesthetic. I think that's what the client is paying for."

Taylor feels computers can complicate the design process, citing the numerous books available to guide users through software manuals as evidence. "The only equipment necessary to create artwork is already on your shoulders," he asserts. "Ideas come from the mind, and you can best refine a piece by taking the time and effort to work with it.

"Computers may drain the creativeness out of a person. For example, relying on a calculator has negatively affected my basic math skills. We tend to forget what we already know. Why should one be creative when the answers are in technology? Often, people won't invent new shapes when shapes are already in the computer."

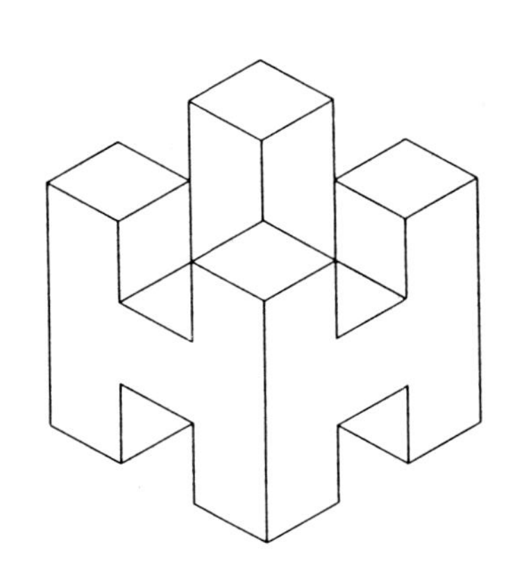

Hastings Development Corp.

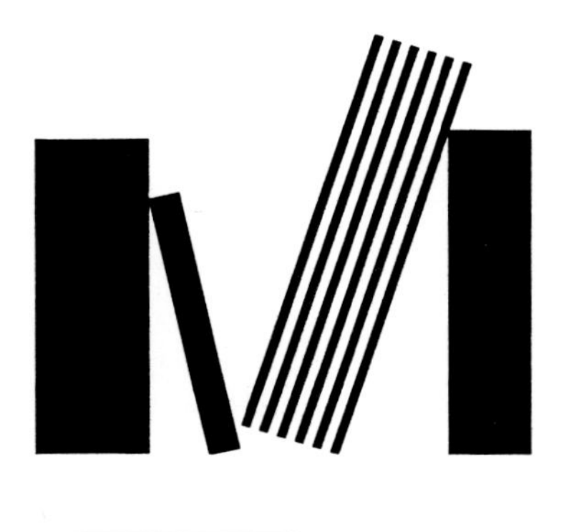

LOGO
Marvelous Books, Inc.

Isler & Isler Contractors

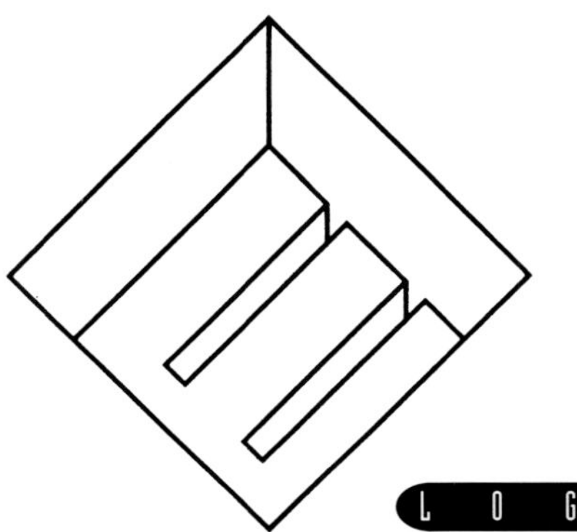

LOGO
Everly Elevator Co.

B is convinced the computer limits ou can produce to the software you buy and the printer you own. "I have thought with paper and pencil for over 39 years in this profession. I maintain what I believe is warmth and style by doing this. Some computer-generated design is so perfect, it is ice-cold.

"I purchase computer services when necessary, but I just don't want to learn a machine. I want to use my hands and mind. Many designers feel that if what they want to do is not in the software, they should try another package or simply give up the concept. I think they should keep talking to and learning from paper people, typographers, printers — avoid becoming a technician."

AIDS Education

POSTER
Hirshhorn Museum's 10th Anniversary

POSTER
Design USA Exhibit/USIA

PeterHaythornthwaiteDesign Ltd.

Auckland, New Zealand

Peter Haythornthwaite

PeterHaythornthwaiteDesign is involved in a broad spectrum of projects that integrate two- and three-dimensional design aspects. With a staff of five, its clients are primarily New Zealand-based. However, the firm also undertakes work in Japan, the United States, and Australia. Principal Peter Haythornthwaite holds a Master of Fine Arts degree from the University of Illinois (USA), and is a Fellow of the Designers Institute of New Zealand. His work has been widely published and the firm has received many awards. These include four 1992 honors from the New Zealand Best Design Awards, as well as awards from Germany's Hanover IF and Frankfurt PLUS.

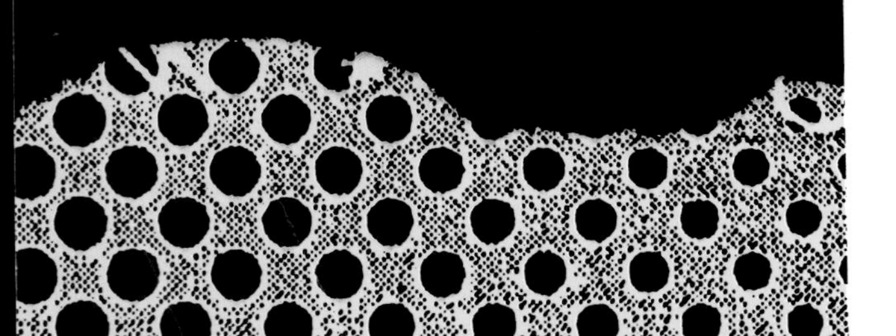

IMMERSION HEATER
Hydrocollator

Crystalite

IDENTITY

Crystalite

BROCHURES

N.Z. Carpet Yarn
Spinners Guild

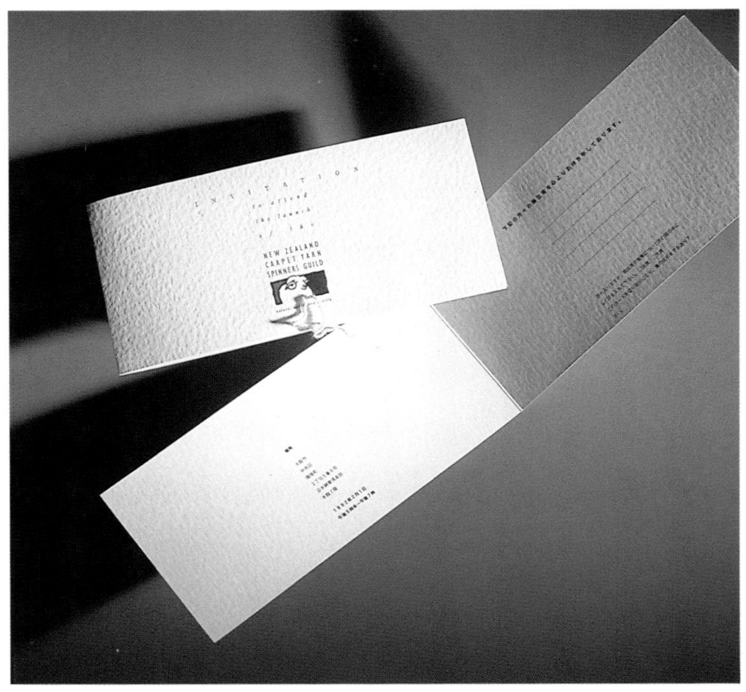

"To me, design first and foremost must be fun," states Peter Haythornthwaite. "I love using the right pencils, paper — I relish working with good typesetters who work as craftsmen. The computer may be a means of pulling back the curtain on idea development."

He does not, however, advocate high expenditures on in-house equipment. "When the dust settles from all the hype, perhaps we'll place the computer in its correct perspective — a wonderful device (of which, no doubt, there are more to come) with some weaknesses. Photocopiers, fax machines, and the like enabled designers to make changes in the way they approach problem solving. The machine is the liberator, not the revolutionary.

"We express our ideas through whatever means is appropriate. Any device for enhancing creativity is fair game — be it scissors and cut paper, photocopy-manipulated images, type, pieces of fabric, light, or color. In our office, we have tended to rely on traditional design techniques. Our contact with electronic technology has mainly been through the use of computer bureaus or scanners. We work with them to create the look we're searching for. This method has enabled us to be creative without getting caught up in trying to work with technology ourselves.

STUDIO STOVE
Oh Ah Stove & Tools

PROMOTIONAL CATALOG
Corporate Gift

"I've been hesitant to enter into this new area because I have seen designers become enamored by the science to the extent that they rely on the technique for results. My method of working is very much a hands-on process. I like to physically manipulate materials and forms. In some way, the computer screen keeps me a distance away from the final result. I enjoy the security of knowing that what I am touching and seeing is based on reality. It is the touch, sound, and sight aspects with which I am very interested.

"This is not to say, however, that I am unaware of or choose to ignore the advantages of technology. In fact, we'll soon be accommodating our studio's first computer dedicated to graphics."

Comset

CATALOG
Technicom

DESK ITEMS
är' ti-fakt-s

PACKAGING
är' ti-fakt-s

PACKAGING
Naturalis Bubble Bath

Pinkhaus Design Corp.

Miami, Florida, USA

Joel Fuller

Joel Fuller is creative director and founder of Pinkhaus Design Corp., the studio that published *The American Directory of Architects* to document the best in U.S. architectural trends. Fuller established his first design firm, Fuller & Friends, in North Carolina. His work has been featured in magazines such as *Print*, *Communication Arts*, and *Graphis*, and numerous books. He has served on *HOW*'s editorial advisory board, on Gilbert Papers' Advisory Council of America — where he co-created "Esse," a line of recycled papers — and has juried many shows, including The Communication Arts Design Show and Logos of the Last Decade.

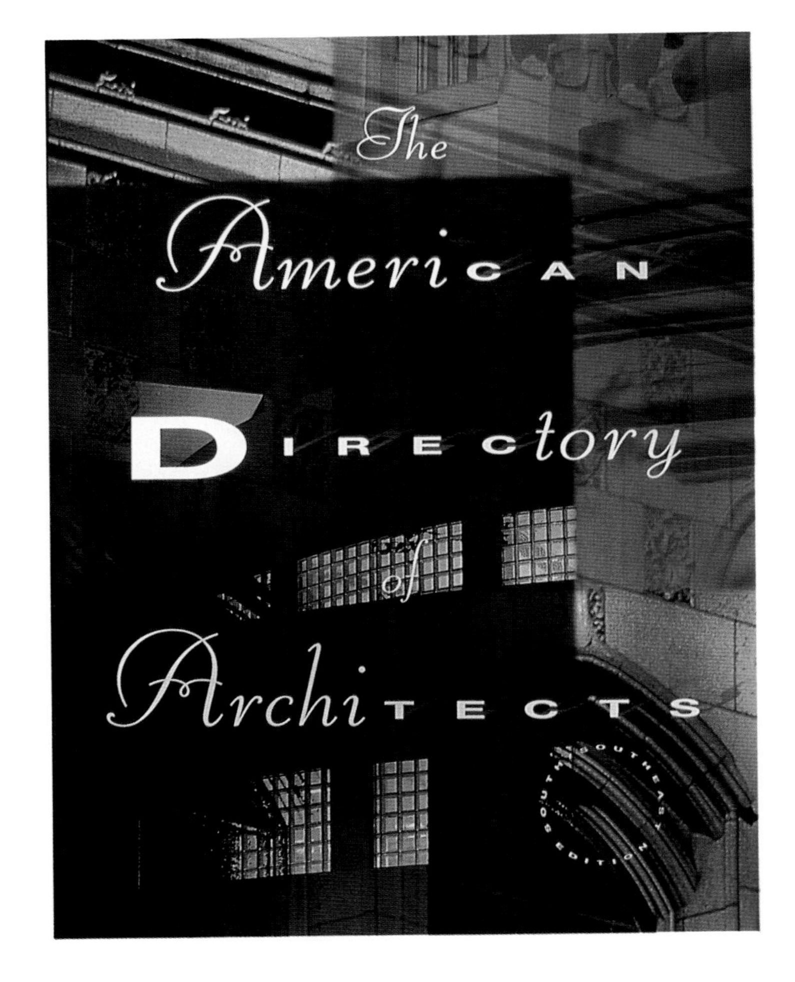

BOOK

American Directory of Architects

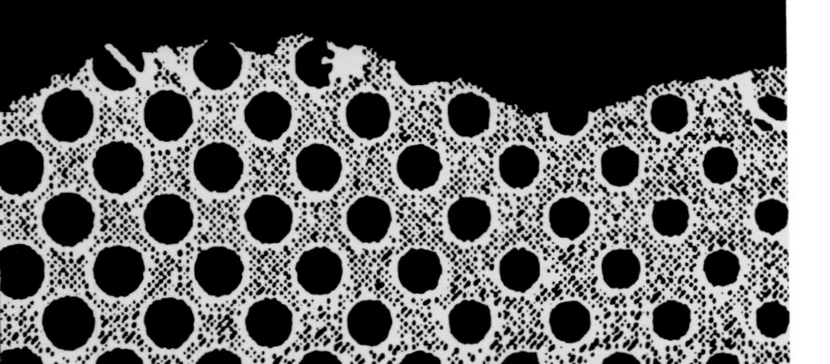

STATIONERY
Pinkhaus Design Corp.

PROMOTION
Gilbert Oxford

COMPACT DISC
Change-It

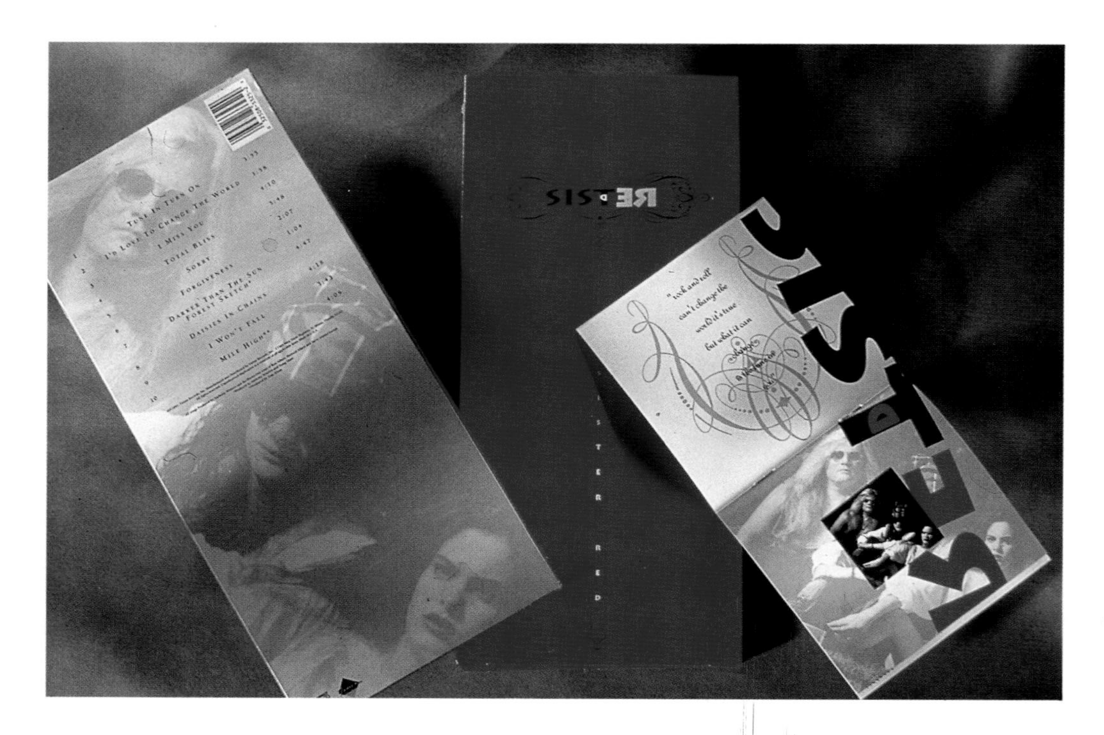

PACKAGING
Sister Red

What is Smart?

That's a good question. And presented here are the responses of our designers. Thirst took an approach that bridges the gap between the sighted and non-sighted world, Pentagram compiled a collection of the smartest rejoinders, Principia Graphica created two visual exercises designed to derail unsmart programmed thinking processes, and Pinkhaus found in their backyard a number of simple, smart solutions to local environmental problems.

Gilbert Designer

Gilbert Esse

"The computer's weakest features are the people using them," states Pinkhaus Design founder Joel Fuller.

"You will never find concepts in computers, and that's what this business is all about. With the explosion of computer typography has come a whole new way of expressing emotions on the printed page. The only problem is that designers can become typesetters, and when that happens, they lose their value to a company as designers." So Fuller issues a warning: "Designers, be careful."

Pinkhaus operates its administrative, database, lead, E-mail, and new business development on computers linked to a local area network with a gateway to remote systems, so the staff can work at home if necessary. Clients can access the Postscript encapsulated version of Pinkhaus computer files to enlarge them, for example, or copy them. Kerning or leading table files and proprietory material are kept confidential.

Fuller gave a lot of thought about how to effectively make the transition into technology. "Early on, I decided that the designers were going to put me out of business trying to learn technology, so I hired a computer-literate person through whom they could channel their work. Eventually, the designers pick up the details on how to use computers. It seems to work well, yet there is always a learning curve to this process.

BROCHURE
Rex

"Because of the mistakes and time needed to learn what works best, we now have production meetings at the beginning of jobs to determine the best way to get it done. Sometimes we decide not to use the computer because of the time involved. One must be intelligent when it comes to technology use. In the end, no one cares whether or not it was designed on a computer. The important thing is, does it communicate what you're trying to communicate?"

General Manager Patrick Fiorentino agrees. "We use computers only to do things that have proven business sense and help us better respond to clients. Some studios think that if they sit at a computer long enough and come up with enough permutations, a great idea will jump out at them, maybe by accident. Our belief is that a good idea should have the proper execution."

"It always gets down to a person and what's inside of them, as opposed to what's inside the program," Fuller summarizes.

STATIONERY
Rex

BROCHURE
African Sailing Safaris

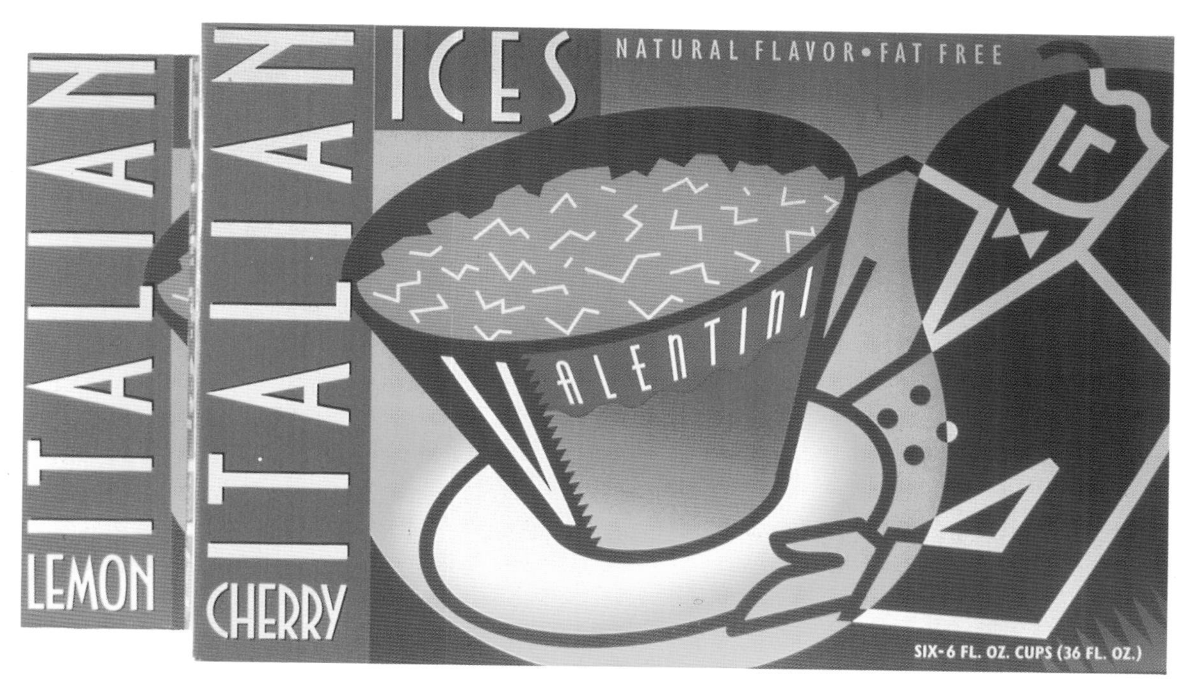

PACKAGING
Valentini Italian Ices

Planet Design Company

Madison, Wisconsin, USA

Dana Lytle and Kevin Wade

Planet Design Company, founded in 1989 by Kevin Wade and Dana Lytle, can already include such well-known firms as Arlington International Racecourse and Miller Brewing Company among its clients. Illinois-born Wade and Lytle, a native of Montana, worked in advertising agencies and design firms before launching Planet. The studio's work has been featured in such publications as *Graphis Design, Graphis Poster, Communication Arts, HOW Self-Promotion, Print's Regional Design Annual, International Logos and Trademarks, Design in Progress,* among others.

BROCHURE
Arlington International Racecourse Ltd.

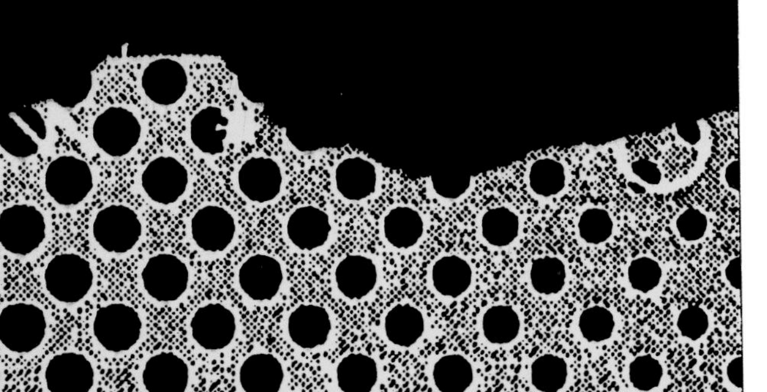

Holding Strong/Madison AIDS Support Network

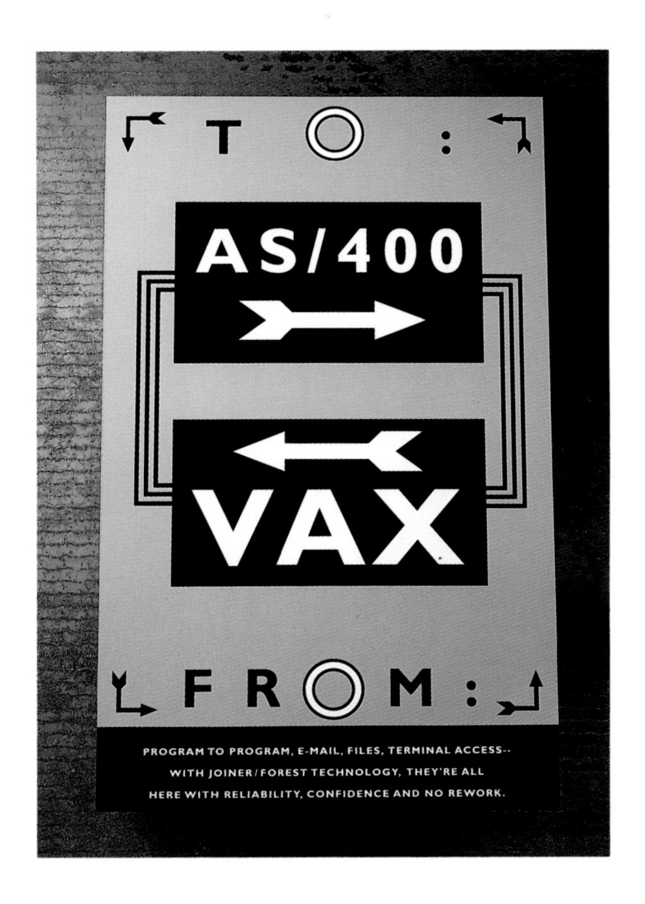

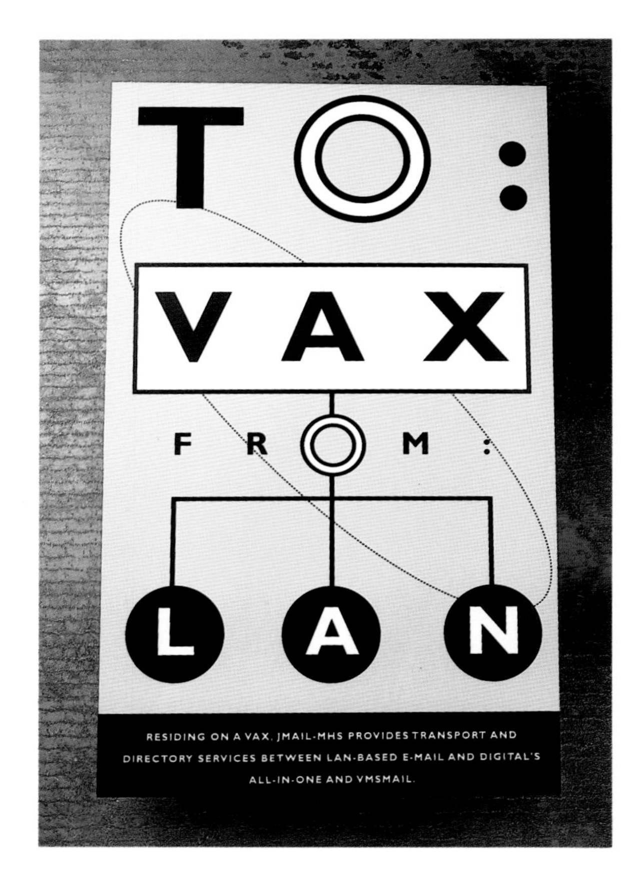

POSTERS

Joiner Software Inc.
(Now Wingra Technologies)

ANNUAL REPORT

Century Communications
Corporations Inc.

"We're getting ready to retire the original Mac we bought in 1989, when Planet Design opened," co-founder Dana Lytle says. "We need more updated capabilities. But it will be hard to see it go."

Lytle and partner Kevin Wade bought that first computer on credit, convinced they'd eventually need it for design, but unsure about its full application. They started by using it as a business machine, tracking jobs, invoices, and so forth. They learned how to adapt it for graphics with a lot of experimentation — and a little help from their friends. "The user's manuals are still in cellophane," Lytle laughs. They now use computers in over half their jobs, mainly for layout, presentations, and initial design. But design concepts are determined "before we hit the computer," says Wade. "We can't focus if we try to design on the computer first."

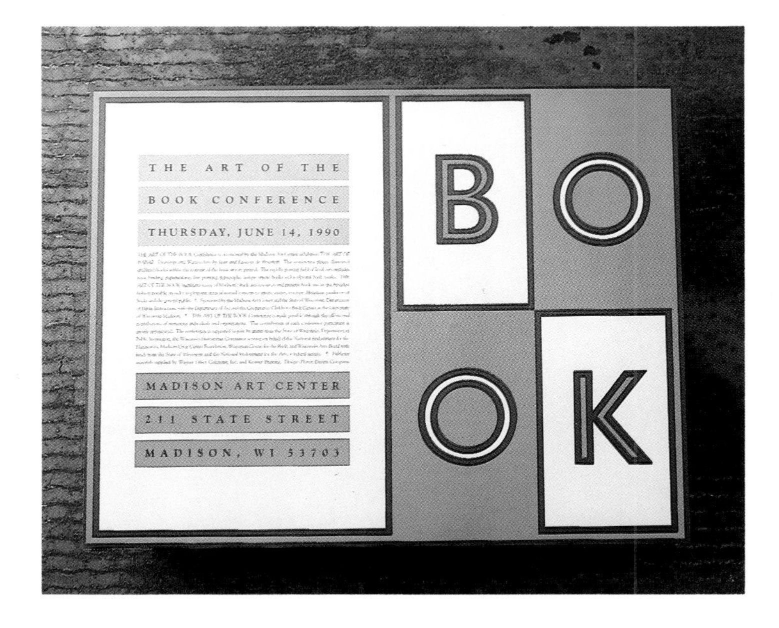

POSTER

Art of the Book

"With computers, we can turn ideas into documents in a matter of hours," says Lytle, but calls technological efficiency a double-edged sword. "The results can be so professional-looking, some designers and clients think a computer is all you need. When you do comps the old-fashioned way, you really see the beauty in the different faces. You can admire the intricacies. On the computer, you lose some of that interaction with type."

With four designers and three workstations, there's some shuffling around for computers, which, Lytle and Wade maintain, are not the answer to all design solutions. Says Wade, "We frequently talk with college students, and have noticed they tend to rely on computers too much. They don't pick up pen, ink, or crayon and work out ideas in another fashion. It concerns me that students may not be getting the schooling in traditional commercial art skills that are valuable to this industry."

Lytle agrees. "There's a lot to be said for pushing some oil pastels around, too."

Freeman Shoe Co. (FSC)

POSTER
American Players Theatre
1991 Season

PROMOTIONAL BOOK
In Toto Fashion

POSTER
Art in Bloom

Barcelona, Spain

Josep Mª Trias

Quod was founded in 1983 under the direction of Esteve Agullo, Jordi Montaña, Mariano Pi, and Josep M. Trias. Today, Quod is made up of 21 professionals in three departments: Industrial and Environmental Design, Graphic Design, and Marketing Consultancy. Its staff is composed of industrial designers, graphic artists, architects, engineers, economists, and business graduates. Trias has exhibited his personal work at trade fairs in Barcelona, Madrid, Milan, and Brussels, as well as in Tokyo and Yokohama, Japan. Studio honors include numerous nominations and awards from ADG/FAD Graphic Design and ADI/FAD Delta.

Cava Chandon

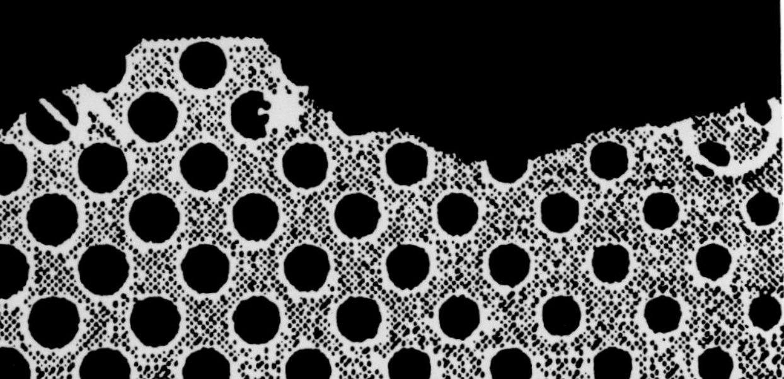

CAMPAIGN
Universitat de Barcelona
Academic Plan

POSTER
Bazar Sos

Pictogrames d'esports

PE 1 Atletisme
PE 2 Bàdminton
PE 3 Bàsquet
PE 4 Beisbol
PE 5 Boxa
PE 6 Ciclisme
PE 7 Esgrima
PE 8 Futbol
PE 9 Gimnàstica
PE 10 Halterofília
PE 11 Handbol
PE 12 Hípica
PE 13 Hoquei herba
PE 14 Judo
PE 15 Lluita
PE 16 Natació
PE 17 Pentatló modern
PE 18 Piragüisme
PE 19 Rem
PE 20 Tennis
PE 21 Tennis taula
PE 22 Tir olímpic
PE 23 Tir amb arc
PE 24 Vela
PE 25 Voleibol
PE 26 Hoquei patins
PE 27 Pilota
PE 28 Taekwondo

Modalitats esportives

PE 29 Natació sincronitzada
PE 30 Salts
PE 31 Waterpolo
PE 32 Piragüisme aigües braves

Pictogramas de deportes

PE 1 Atletismo
PE 2 Badminton
PE 3 Baloncesto
PE 4 Beisbol
PE 5 Boxeo
PE 6 Ciclismo
PE 7 Esgrima
PE 8 Fútbol
PE 9 Gimnasia
PE 10 Halterofilia
PE 11 Balonmano
PE 12 Hípica
PE 13 Hockey hierba
PE 14 Judo
PE 15 Lucha
PE 16 Natación
PE 17 Pentatlón moderno
PE 18 Piragüismo
PE 19 Remo
PE 20 Tenis
PE 21 Tenis mesa
PE 22 Tiro olímpico
PE 23 Tiro con arco
PE 24 Vela
PE 25 Voleibol
PE 26 Hockey patines
PE 27 Pelota
PE 28 Taekwondo

Modalidades deportivas

PE 29 Natación sincronizada
PE 30 Saltos
PE 31 Waterpolo
PE 32 Piragüismo aguas bravas

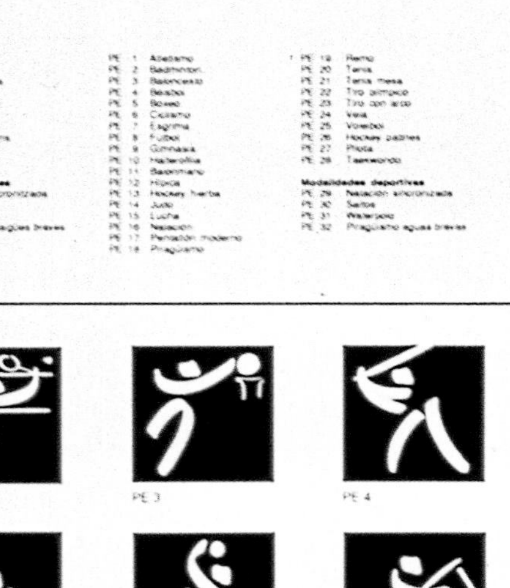

Barcelona '92 Olympic Games

SIGNAGE SYSTEM
Barcelona '92 Olympic Games

POSTER
Official Symbol, Barcelona '92 Olympic Games

POSTER
Barcelona '92 Olympic Games

Josep M. Trias, who manages Quod's Department of Graphic Design, has some candid views about technology in commercial art. "It is difficult for me to believe that a modern, competitive, research-based studio exists that doesn't use computers as an everyday instrument of work," he says. "Computers are extraordinary devices that designers must serve.

Designers may have to serve machines, but only to reap their benefits in what Trias sees as a symbiotic relationship. "We have to control the computer and its programs to translate our thoughts about a project into a workable format. In design, computers do not have limits."

Trias also feels strongly about the potential of machines. "I think the computer is an instrument that permits a variety of shapes, textures, colors, perspectives, volumes, and animation that it would be impossible to achieve using craftwork methods. But computers are silly and stupid. Only a good designer can do a good design using computers; a bad designer in front of a computer will create a still worse design. In an ideal world, computers would always be dominated by the designer. But sometimes the opposite is true. A computer still does not solve the problem of creativity.

"In our studio, we use the computer to do layouts with proofs, change colors, and produce artwork, but we do not use it for presentations. I believe the traditional methods produce presentations with a superior quality compared to those done by the computer printer.

"Quod's seven designers first have to be traditionally skilled to be technological designers. We believe design cannot be left to intuition; it must be a combination of creativity, competitive strategy, and market research. But to improve, we work constantly with the computer — the theory without practice is meaningless."

La Recerca a Catalunya,
Repte de Futur

Punt de Servei

POSTER
No Fugis d'Estudi

POSTER
Cap a la Reforma

Reactor Art and Design, Ltd.

Toronto, Ontario, Canada

Louis Fishauf

Reactor Art and Design, Ltd., was co-founded in 1982 by Louis Fishauf and Bill Grigsby. Reactor provides graphic design and illustration to clients in Canada and the U.S., and represents an international roster of 26 artists working in traditional and digital media. In 1991, Fishauf received the Les Usherwood Award from the Art Directors Club of Toronto. This award is presented to one person each year in recognition of a lifetime of excellence in communication arts. Among his other awards, Fishauf also earned 10 Gold and 10 Silver National Magazine Awards for cover design, art direction, and illustration. Reactor's work has been featured in many publications, including *Novum Gebrauchgraphik* (Germany), *BàT* (France) and *Idea* (Japan).

POSTER
Happy Face

POSTER
Adobe Venus
(Illustrator 4 for Windows)

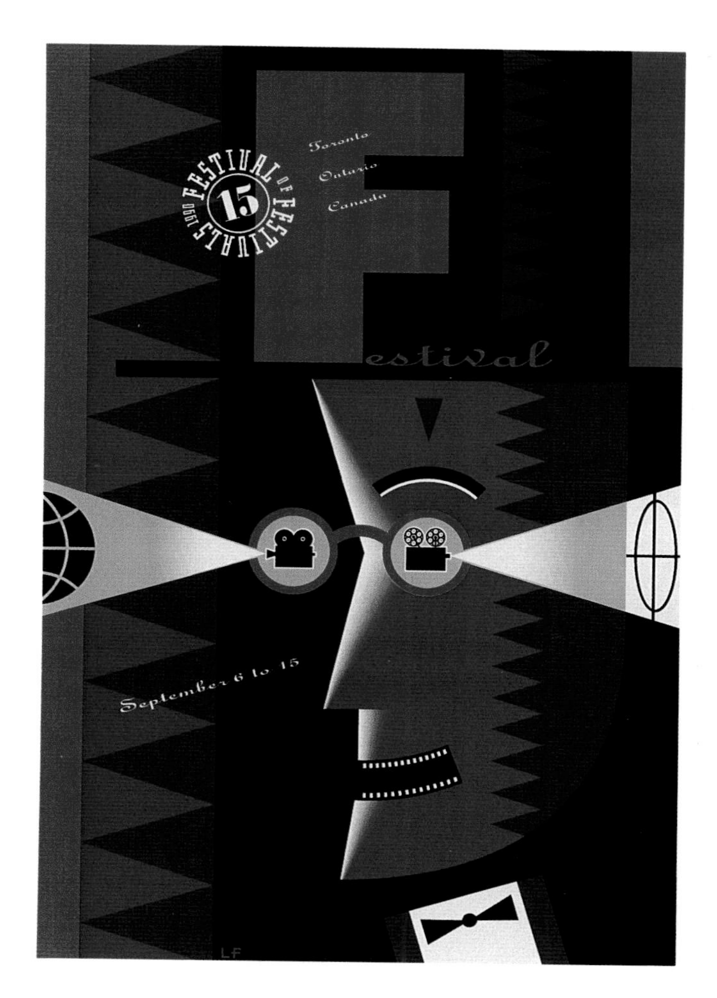

POSTER
Festival of Festivals 90

Q.P. Doll

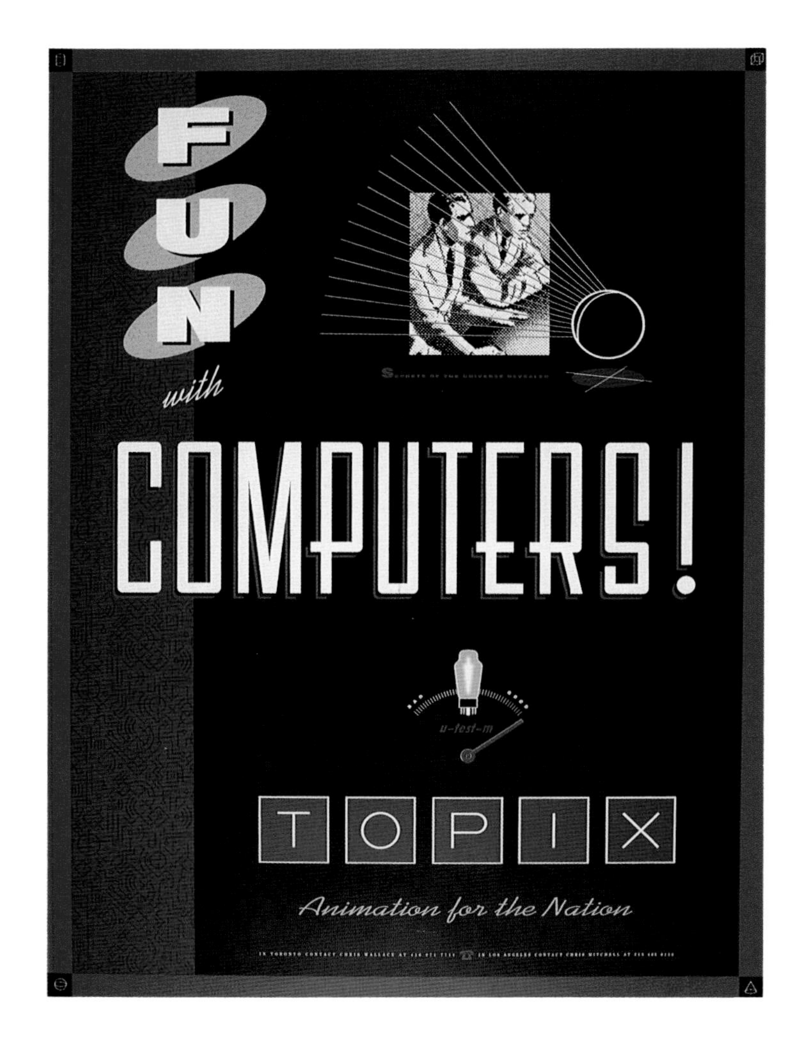

R.E.M.

POSTER
Fun with Computers

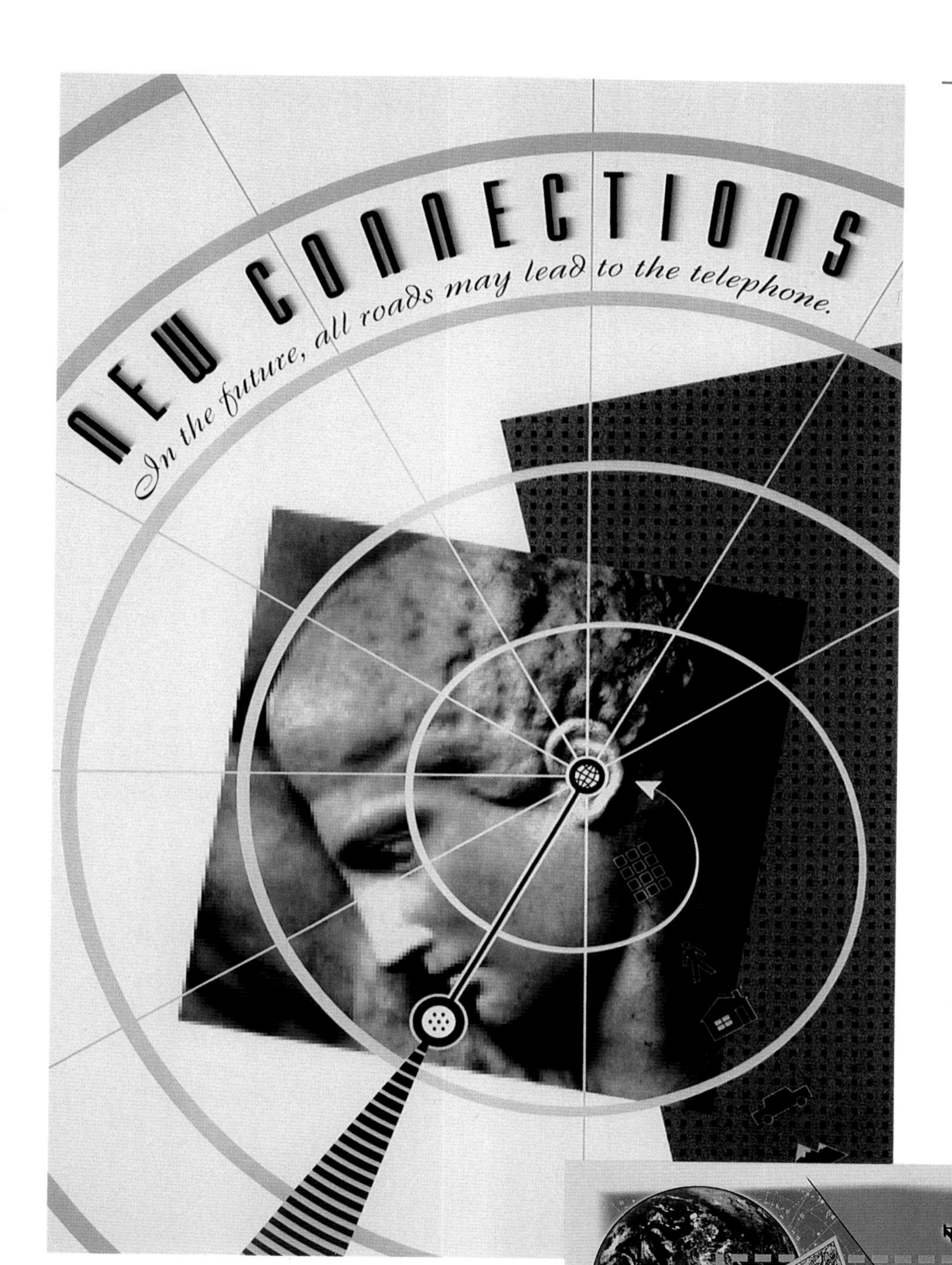

POSTER
New Connections

POSTER
Mapping Software

Louis Fishauf, co-founder of Reactor Art and Design, often prefers the non-hectic environment of working at home, and computers have been critical in supporting his electronic mobility. "A call to the studio and I receive files via modem," he says. "98 percent of our work uses a computer in some way. Computers let you create any design you want, as long as you can learn the software."

He feels strongly about technology's value. "Design in terms of mass communications or printing is computer design now. In fact, it's surprising that a book like this is even being done these days."

Computers are Fishauf's gateway to illustration, animation, and, further down the road, virtual reality. "Maybe I'll create a 3-D virtual world someday." But he will admit to drawbacks: "You can tend to get too focused on the screen. Interacting with people, on the other hand, helps to recharge your battery. You absorb from the real world and reinterpret it at the computer."

With a predisposition for things technological, Fishauf was able to teach himself the software and purchase compatible hardware. "I've always been interested in computer ability and the electronic generation of imagery, and I rely on dealers for advice. "Software can be difficult to learn, and it's getting more specialized all the time. It was simpler when I first got involved about six years ago. Now it's more difficult to keep up and master more than three or four programs.

I'm playing with 3-D modeling now, but I especially enjoy creating single-image projects like posters. I like the scale of posters and the boldness."

Inspirit 90

Plague Doctor

POSTER
Design Essentials

Power to the Planet

Client/Server

Signals Design Group Inc.

Vancouver, British Columbia, Canada

Gus Tsetsekas

Gus Tsetsekas was born in Greece, grew up in Toronto, and moved to Vancouver in 1981, where he gives equal time to his design firm, Signals Design Group, and a lifestyle that includes travel, cycling, and hiking. "When I first moved to Vancouver, I was very career-oriented, to the exclusion of all else. With partner David Young and a handful of talented employees, we built Signals into a successful firm, but at a price to our personal lives that I found too high." The two partners agreed to an amicable split and Signals was downsized in 1990. Tsetsekas is the recipient of numerous awards, and has had over 90 projects receive worldwide recognition in publications such as *Successful Logos Worldwide* and *The AIGA Annual*.

COMPACT DISCS

A) Silverman, B) Bach Children's Chorus, and C) Watmough

LOGO
Canadian HIV Trials Network

LOGO
Rouvain Recordings

Curio Concert Series

POLICY PAMPHLETS
Elite Insurance

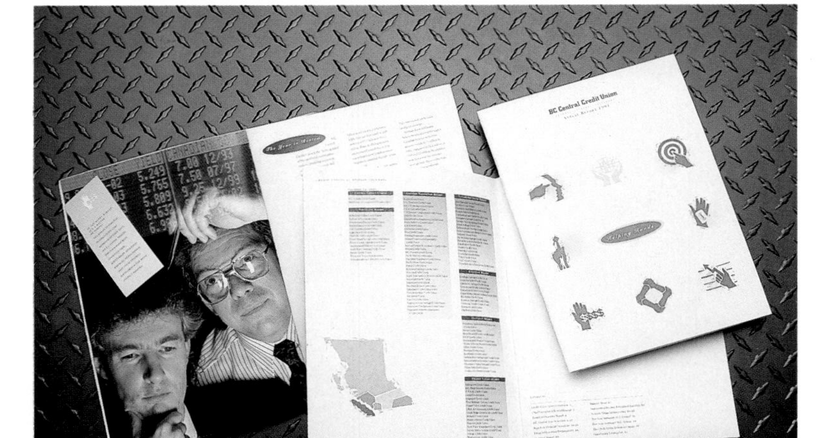

ANNUAL REPORT
BC Central Credit Union

COMMEMORATIVE STAMP
Canada Post

PROMOTIONAL
1993 World Choral Symposium

"For me, the computer has been a godsend," says Gus Tsetsekas, principal of Signals Design Group. "It allows me unimagined control of my work and a tremendous increase in productivity. I can now do more work for cultural and non-profit organizations who previously could not afford our services. I've also streamlined my business so that I spend less time managing and supervising and more time designing.

"The computer's strength is in its potential to change the way we conceive and carry out our work. In the future, I imagine more of the technical know-how will be built into the software. Functions such as kerning, trapping, and color reproduction will become transparent to the user, freeing a creative person from being a technical jack-of-all-trades to concentrate on the creative process. Software will be more sensitive to my needs and adapt to my idiosyncracies, rather than me adapting to it. I see a day when we will interface with computers as simply as we use a pen today."

ANNUAL REVIEW
Asia Pacific Foundation

Like many traditional artists, Tsetsekas intuitively relies on his own two hands for specific tasks. "I can draw calligraphic forms very easily with a brush and ink, but I can drive myself crazy trying to achieve the same thing with a computer. However, I can scan my ink drawing and easily convert it to an electronic format that can be adjusted or manipulated later.

"When we converted our production services to computer, we quickly realized we needed additional skills internally, which we had previously taken for granted. For instance, proofing for copy accuracy became our responsibility rather than the typesetter's. It's true that technology is still quite primitive and far less intuitive than it should be. However, as technical improvements are made, I'm hopeful we'll see a seamless integration of software across all platforms in the not-too-distant future."

Design Week

Vancouver Opera

Siobhan Keaney Design

London, England

Siobhan Keaney

Siobhan Keaney graduated from the London College of Printing in 1982 with a B.A. in Graphic Design. After some design consultancies, she became an independent designer in 1985. Keaney's work has been published in every D&AD Annual since 1982, in books such as *The Encyclopaedia of British Graphic Designers, Typography Now: The New Wave,* and *International Women in Design,* and in magazines like *Graphis, Communication Arts,* and *Blueprint.* Awards include a D&AD Commendation for an annual report in 1991 and two D&AD Silver Awards in 1990. She has exhibited her work at galleries, museums, and universities in London, Moscow, Tokyo, New York, Los Angeles, and Offenbach, Germany.

CHRISTMAS CARD
The Mill

ANNUAL REPORT

Apicorp

BROCHURE COVER

Seymour Powell

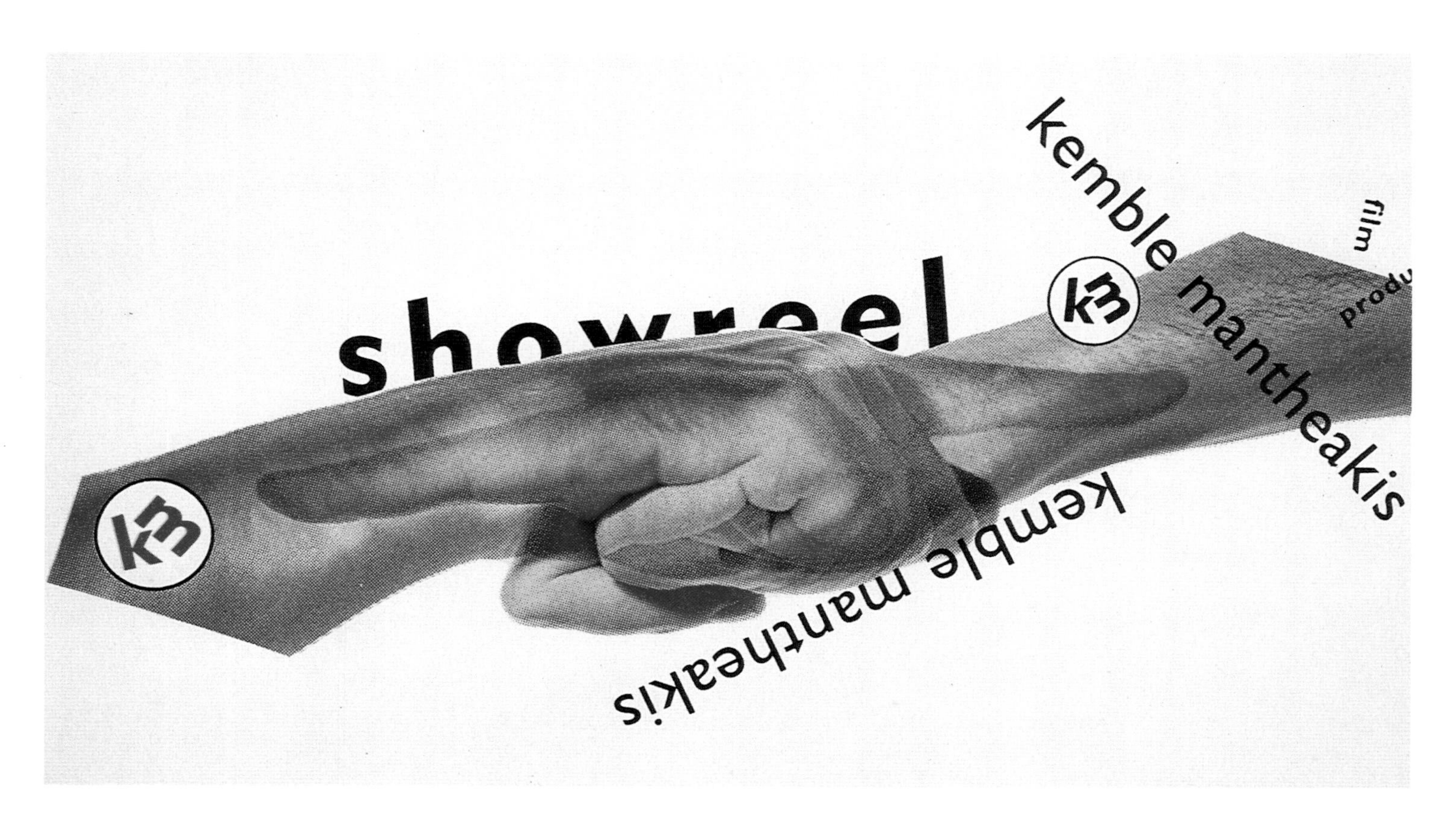

PROMOTION
Kemble Mantheakis

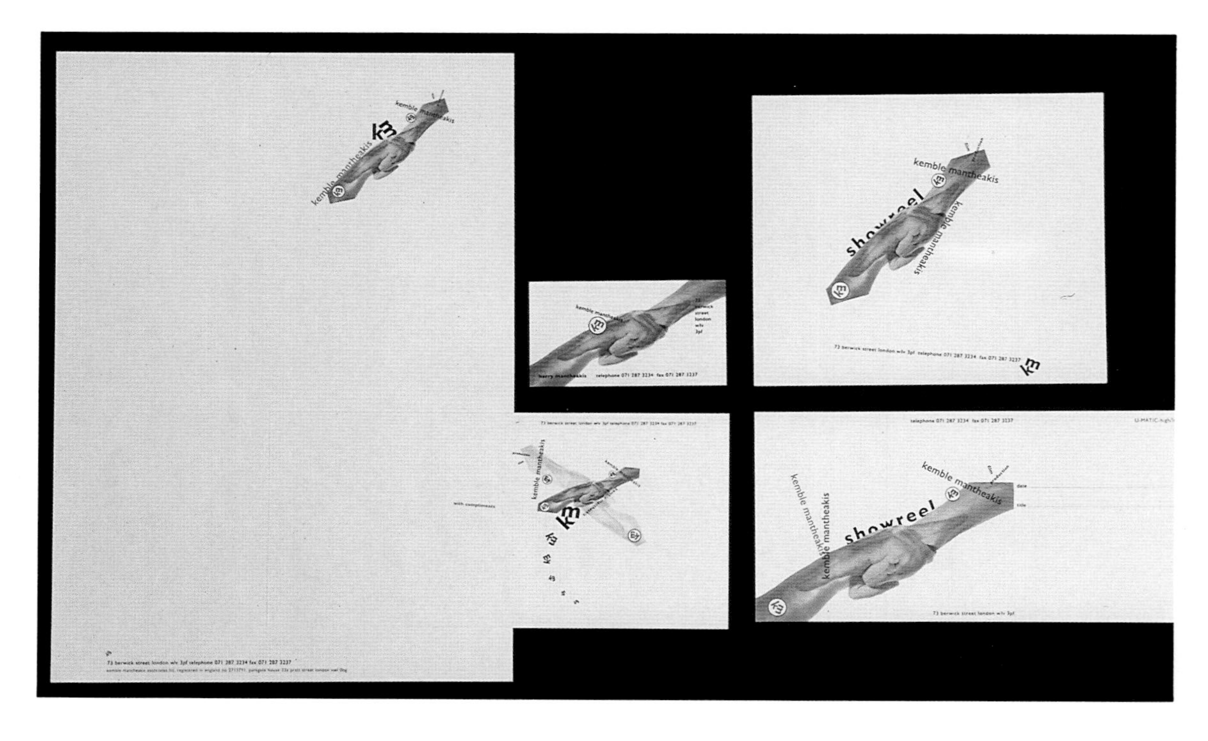

STATIONERY
Kemble Mantheakis

ALBUM COVER
What Are Dreams Made Of

Siobhan Keaney's introduction to computers was three or four hours with a computer consultant — "and it put me off because it was dull," she states. "I kept asking, can it do this, or this? And the answer was always, you must buy more programs. It took so long to do simple things."

Keaney thinks her initial computer struggle may have had something to do with her "natural defense mechanism against technology." She says, "The computer is a slightly alien thing. It's obviously here to stay, but I see no reason why everyone should be Mac'd up. I find it unfortunate that so many clients have fallen into the seduction of computers. I have a computer in the studio, but there's a lot on it I've never used. I like to touch paper instead.

"People get confused by experimentation with technology that doesn't have anything to do with creativity. When you're hand-drawing type, you're deciding everything about it. When there's not much type to a project, I prefer hand-rendering it, mostly because of the texture achieved. For headlines, or type that stands out, I prefer drawings because your individual personality comes out more favorably through your work. On the computer, there's only a few routes you can take that everyone is already taking.

"For example, take a pencil to paper and you can make one mark; take a softer pencil, and you create another mark — the possibilities are endless. Computers don't have that variation in them — they cannot logically be that different.

"I believe eventually designers will start demanding more from software companies instead of being force-fed the corporate concept of graphic needs. Sometimes I wonder if this explosion of technology is not part of a huge marketing plan, where some corporations let technology out a little at a time, and use designers as guinea pigs to see what sells."

BROCHURES & POSTERS

90-Day Access, High Rate of Interest

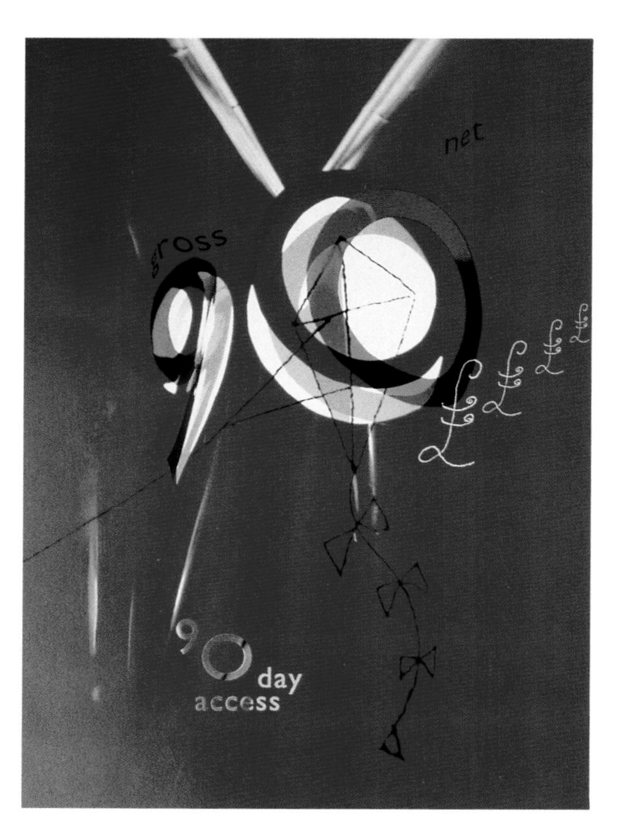

Apicorp

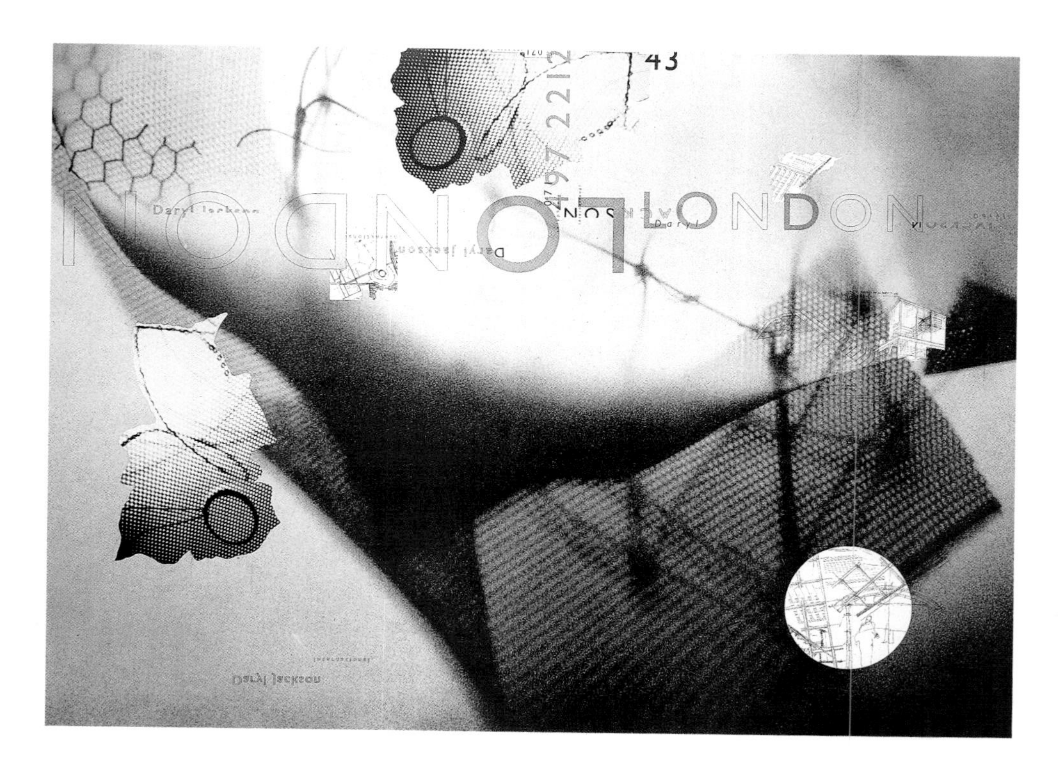

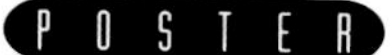

Daryl Jackson International,
Architects

Spatchurst Design Associates

Darlinghurst, New South Wales, Australia

John Spatchurst and Stephen Joseph

John Spatchurst and Steven Joseph formed Spatchurst Design Associates (SDA) in 1984. Spatchurst has worked with many major cultural organizations in his state of New South Wales, producing publications, posters, and exhibitions. Among his accomplishments, Spatchurst was responsible for the Arnott's exhibition at Australia's Powerhouse Museum. He is a Fellow of the Design Institute of Australia and his work is regularly published in both Australian and international publications. Steven Joseph's architectural background was critical in the design of major signage systems for the National Library of Australia and the State Library and Art Gallery of New South Wales, among others. In 1991, SDA opened an Asian office in Singapore.

INVITATION

The Magic of the Paris Opera

Lucian Freud

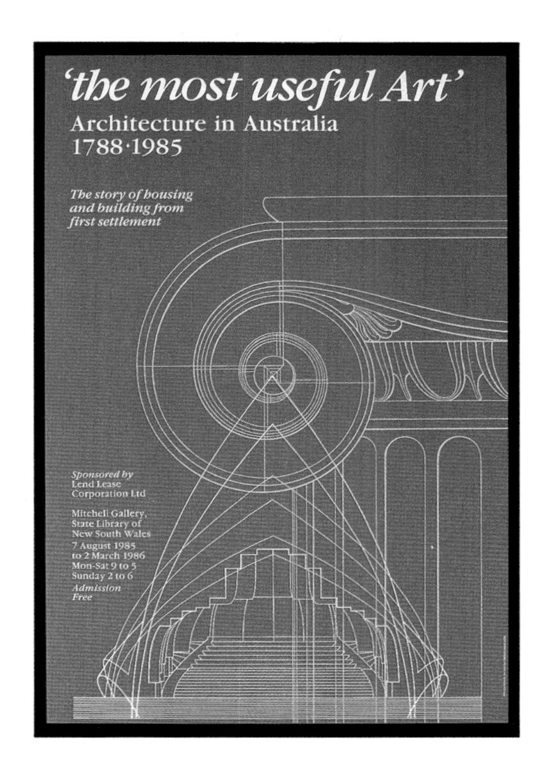

EXHIBITION POSTER

the most useful Art

STATIONERY

Various Identities

AWARD
Workgroup of the Year

"In this century, the design developments of each generation have reflected the technology of production," states John Spatchurst. "Innovators have always pushed the limits of technology, and in doing so, changed the process and visual language for all time."

Spatchurst sees both sides of the computer design issue. "As communicators, we have to speak a language appropriate to the era. However good our ideas may be, if they are expressed in an outmoded form, they'll be ignored and considered irrelevant. This poses a dilemma for us as designers. New technology is very powerful. It is easy to be seduced by its versatility and seemingly endless choice. But, while acknowledging its potential, we must step back and impose our own will, rather than be led blindly by technology."

ANNUAL REPORT
Westmead Hospital

Partner Steven Joseph recognizes that machines can be unwelcome interlopers in the process of innovation. "Computers can restrain creative design. Designers become limited by losing track of the larger picture. Some designers also restrict themselves when they adapt to the parameters of the Mac environment; they stop designing solutions that cannot be produced on the computer. Or the designer begins using elements just because they can be done on the Mac, regardless of whether or not they are actually appropriate to the project."

"As we develop concepts, we find technology assumes a greater role," Spatchurst asserts. "Computers allow us to explore alternatives at a far greater speed than before, while they closely approximate skills of the finished artist. Another benefit is that, previously, the somewhat tedious but critical phases of alignments, keylines, trappings, and registration can now be easily locked in. These advantages of in-house technology may have increased our studio's responsibilities, but they have also made us more responsive to client needs."

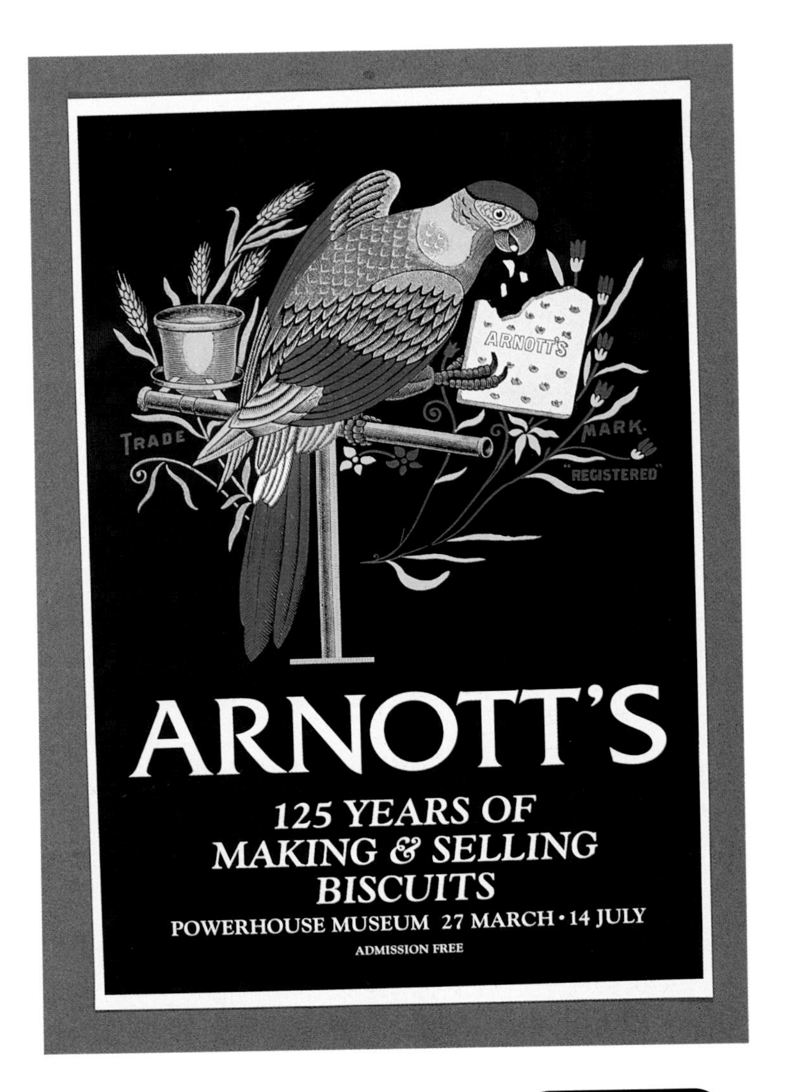

Arnott's

BROCHURE
Australasian Wheels for the Mind

Sydney Olympic 2000 Bid

STATE LIBRARY
OF NEW SOUTH WALES

State Library of New South Wales

BROCHURE

from Australia

Steven R. Gilmore Design

Vancouver, British Columbia, Canada

Steven Gilmore

Kevin Westenberg

Steven Gilmore, a self-taught artist with no formal training, designed his first record sleeve for a Vancouver-based alternative band in 1980. Since then, he has created hundreds more sleeves for record labels such as EMI, Capitol, Geffen, Warner Bros., and PolyGram. Gilmore's design has been recognized with honors from organizations such as CASBY, West Coast Music, and the Art Directors Club of Los Angeles. His work has appeared in publications worldwide, including *HOW, Publish, Design Journal* (Korea), and *Emigre,* and in numerous music periodicals. Gilmore has recently expanded his design efforts into household furnishings.

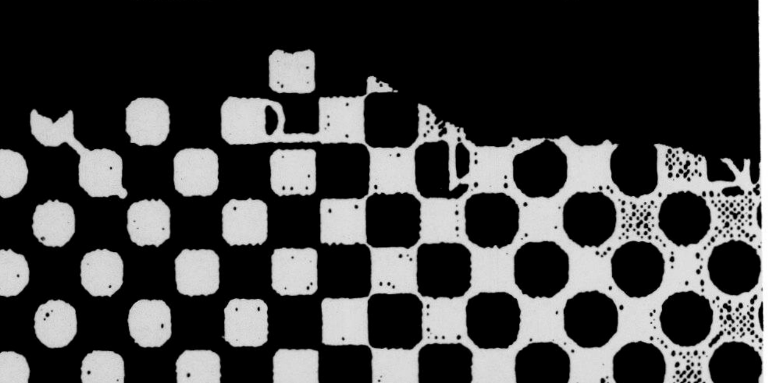

POSTER
Decades

POSTER
Vivienne Mackinder

BROCHURE
PFS Engineering

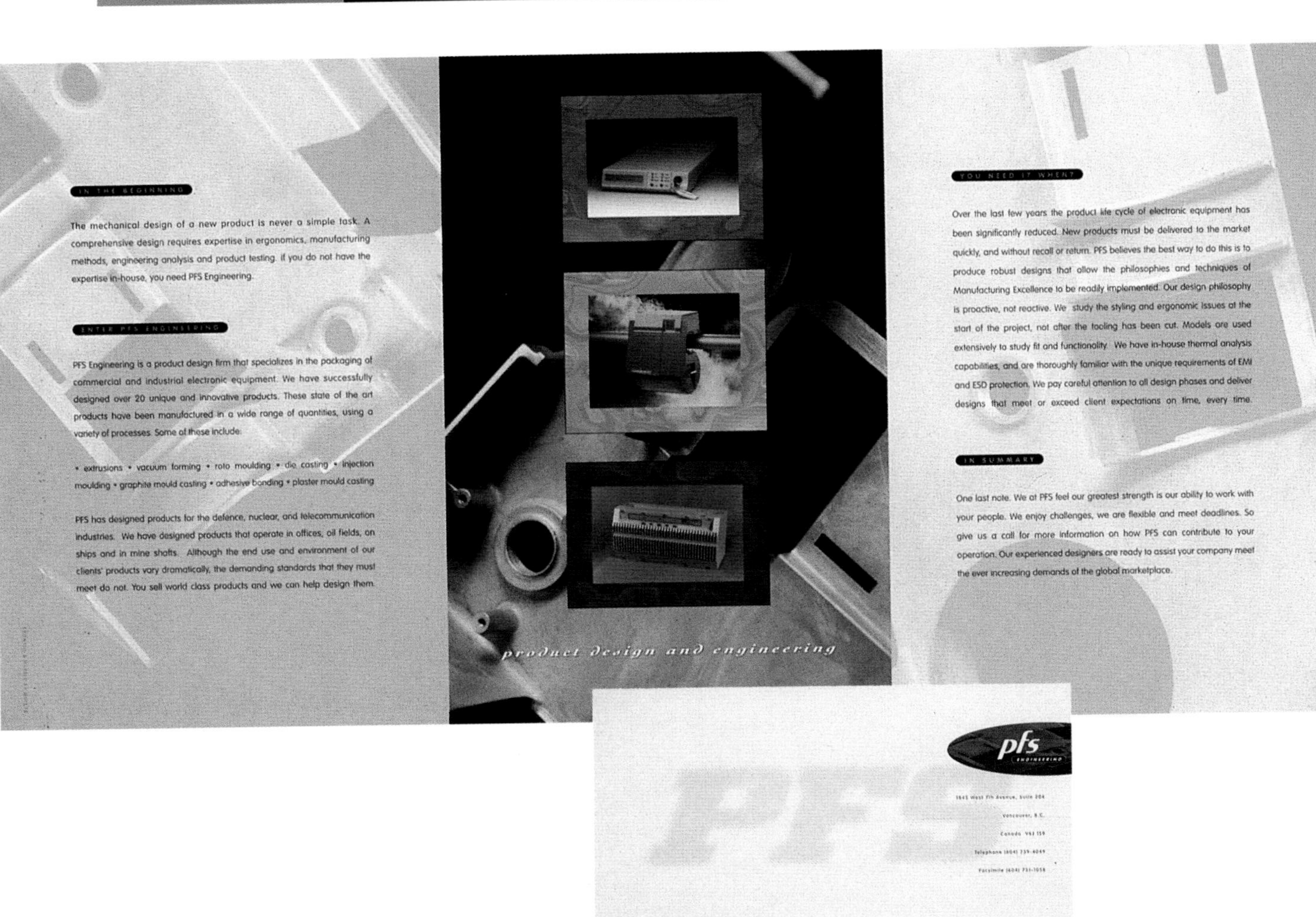

pfs
ENGINEERING
PFS

STATIONERY
PFS Engineering

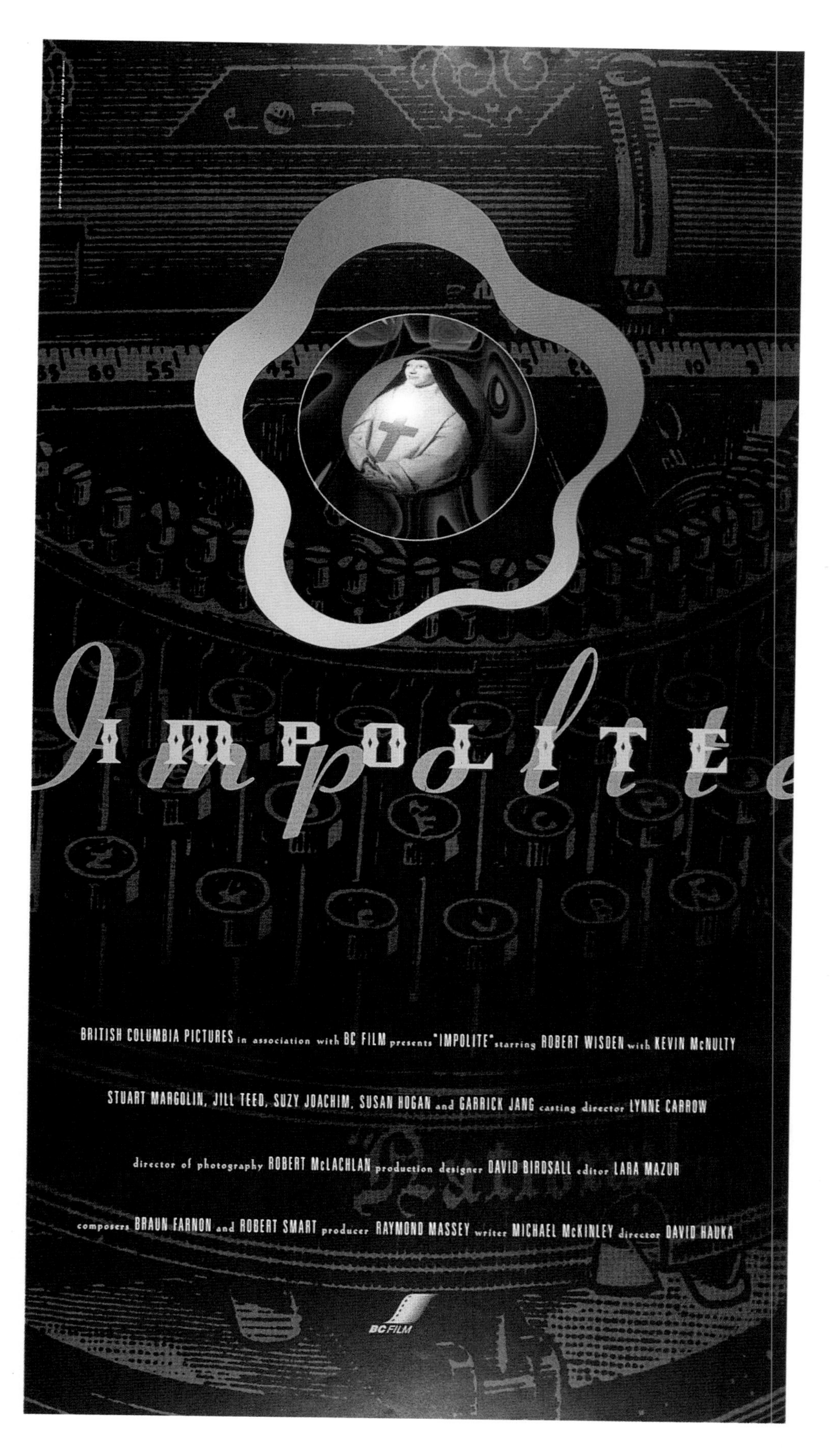

"The computer?" Steven Gilmore is certain. "I couldn't live without it, that's for sure."

Gilmore is a painter who once created his graphics work by hand. "I'd speak to Neville Brody every so often and he'd say, 'Haven't you got a computer yet?' Then one day I got a typesetting bill for $5,000, although I'd spec'd the type so carefully there was no room for mistakes. I realized I could buy my own Mac for less than that, so I did. The typesetter was reinterpreting my work, anyway.

"I learned technology through trial and error. It was painful at first — at least 16 hours a day for a month, without manuals. But I like perfection, so the actual creative transition was natural. And I can still do a lot of freehand-ish type of design, like script, on the computer.

"Technology hasn't changed my work much. Some clients thought my old work was computer-generated, and they don't seem to care how I produce it. It's not faster, actually; I probably spend more time on projects now than I used to, because there's so many more options. But I think my graphics have improved. For example, without computers, if I picked certain colors that didn't work well together, I couldn't change them if time was limited or the budget was tight. Now I can get a good idea of how colors will work with each other in advance."

Impolite

POSTER
Visual Aid

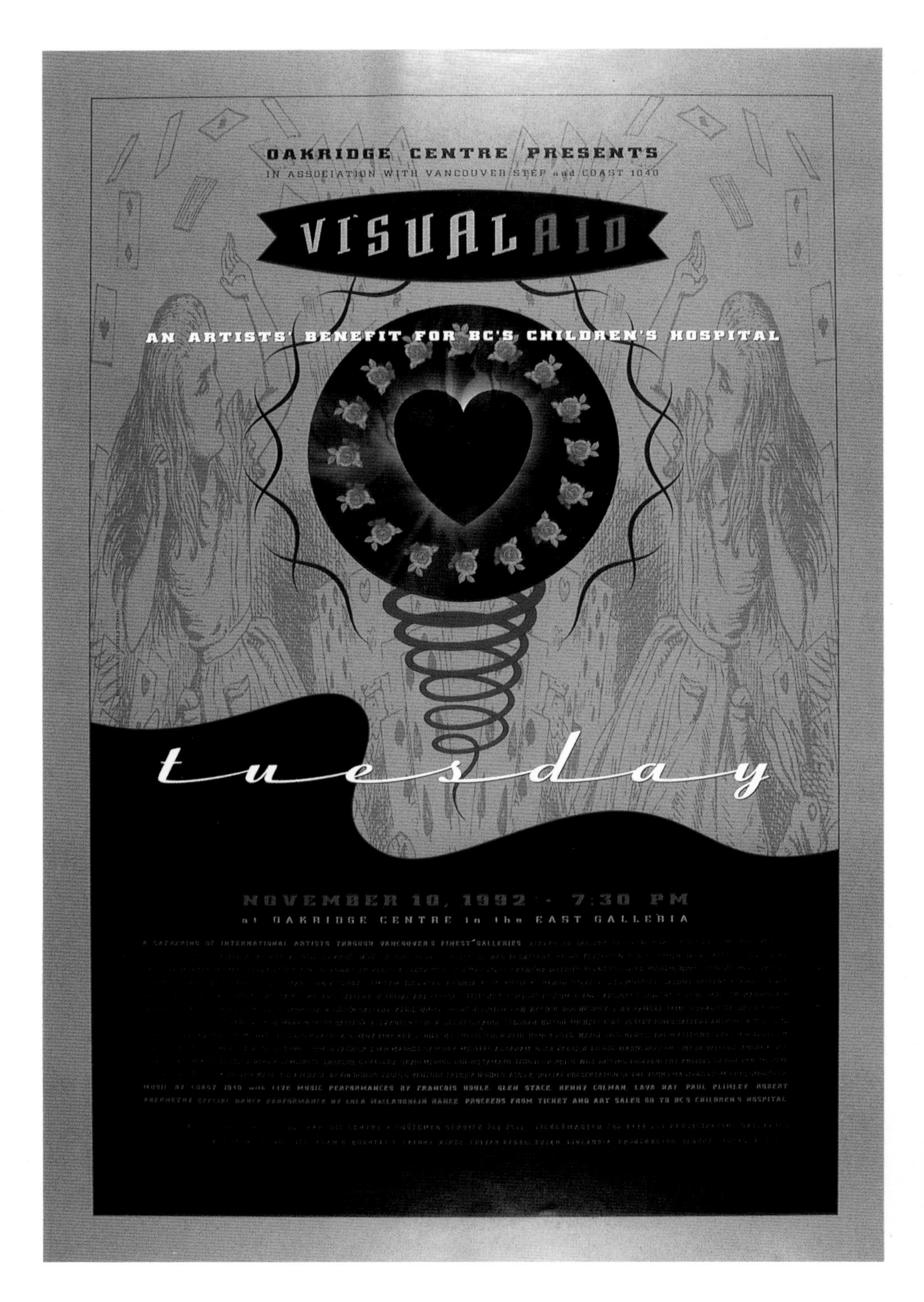

Gilmore, the fine artist, is proud of his commercial work, but recognizes the difference. "Although I would show my graphic work in a gallery — and I do believe graphic design is just as creative as any other art — it is created to be printed on papers and surfaces that are not archival. Even if the graphic information is stored on computer disk, it will eventually be lost. The medium is that volatile. With my oil paintings, on the other hand, I know they will be around long after I'm gone.

"Programmers still need to work on color calibration. What you see on the screen at home and at a color bureau is usually dissimilar. I've learned to use colors that compensate for the difference in the screen interpretation and the actual output. Otherwise, I don't see that there's any limits at all to computers, except they won't take photographs or paint . . . yet."

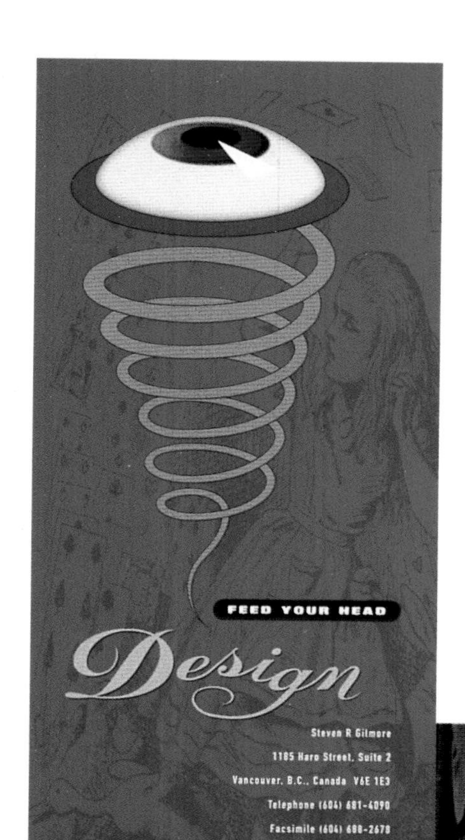

PROMOTIONAL CARD
"Feed Your Head"

PROMOTIONAL CARD
"I had too much to dream last night"

PROMOTIONAL CARD
"taste the whip in love not given lightly"

Rose and Thorn

Studio M D

Seattle, Washington, USA

Glenn Mitsui, Jesse Doquilo, and Randy Lim

Studio M D's trademark is a multi-dimensional style of art called "interactive print design." They believe the shapes, folds, and the detailed content of their work heightens viewer perception and increases retention. Among its major milestones, they designed the product launch materials for Aldus PageMaker 4.0 and the package illustration for a new Aldus product, Fetch; cosmetic ski designs for PRE Skis; a line of T-shirts produced under their own label, "Republic of Design;" a 30' x 20' holiday sculpture for the Sea-Tac International Airport; and editorial illustrations for *MacWorld* magazine and Bantam Books.

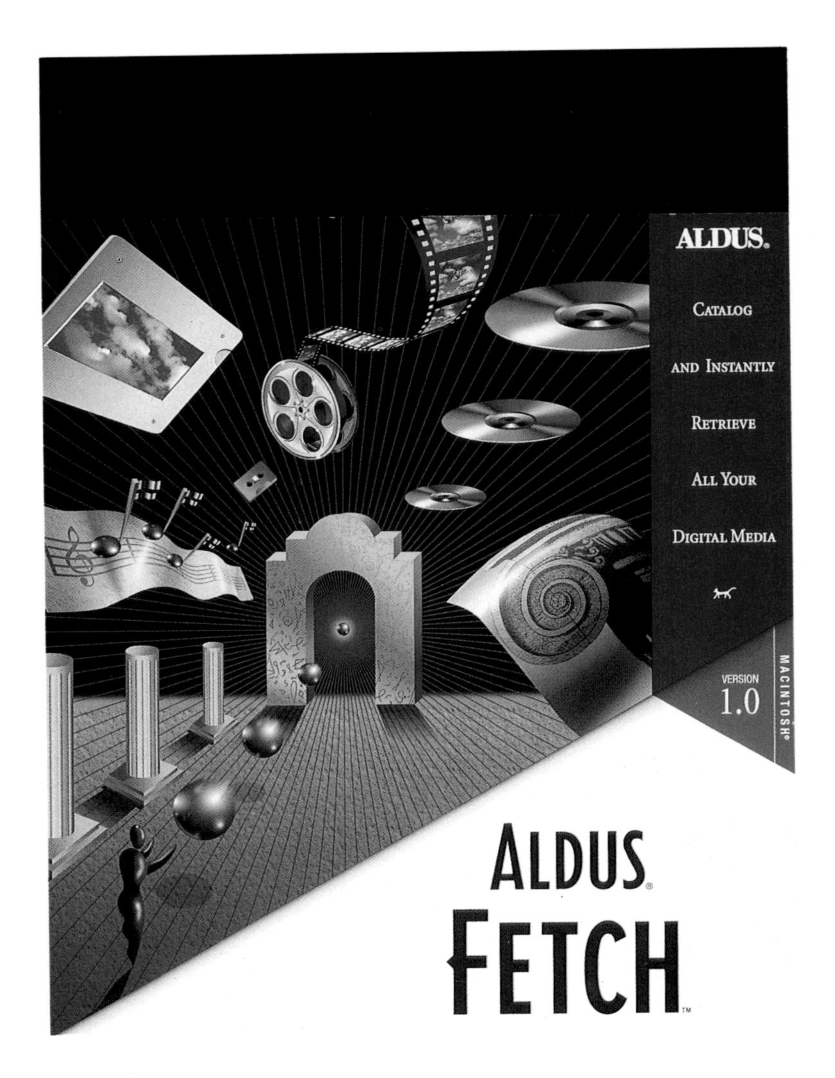

ILLUSTRATION
Aldus Fetch

HOLIDAY SCULPTURE
Sea-Tac International Airport

POSTER
The First Trapeze Awards

"Computers have made our company independent," says Glenn Mitsui, one of the three Studio M D partners. "We rarely go out of the studio. We use computers for practically everything — estimates, illustration, marketing, and tracking job time." The give-and-take of the computer evolution has had its effect on Studio M D. Their responsibilities in rendering a finished product have not only increased, but expanded into other disciplines. But the significance of technology to their bottom line was undeniable.

"It was an easy decision to incorporate computers into the business. That was the niche we were going after; we evaluated our market when we first started, and 90% of it was high-tech. Technical companies wanted designers who used their software packages, who talked the same language they do. For example, we've gotten jobs developing icons because we're known as 'computer people.' Now we even send out an interactive disk to prospective clients as part of our portfolio. We broke into *MacWorld* magazine with that technique."

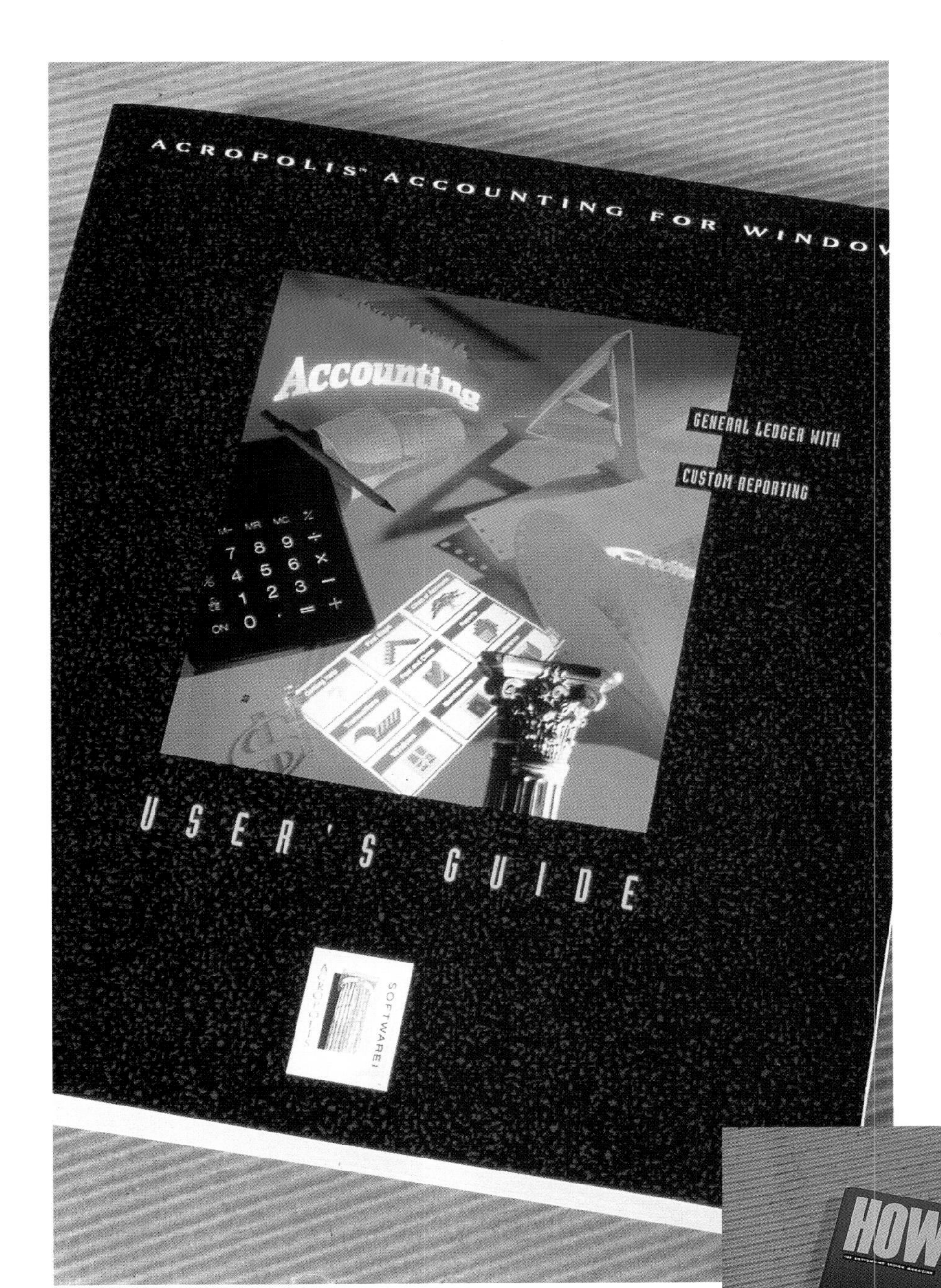

USER'S GUIDE
Acropolis Accounting Software

ILLUSTRATION
HOW Business Annual '93

They adapt computer-aided design to make it look "friendlier." "We incorporate handmade textures, for example, with ink and a brush." Co-founder Jesse Doquilo adds, "We're constantly upgrading our computers for more speed or memory. We keep the cost down because our machines are already configured for what we'll need in the future, which will probably tend toward multi-media." Randy Lim, who does the estimates, doesn't think it's realistic to incorporate the cost of upgrades into their service fees. "With our upgrades comes the ability to do more and become more efficient, so the cost of new equipment quickly equals out with increased productivity."

"Our only limitation is the time it takes to experiment," says Mitsui. "We've had to learn to compress the time frame for a job to be profitable. So we have to do the best job we can, and that means quickly mastering the software to do the project."

Tony Gable and 206

Talk 'n Trash

POSTER

Seattle Tech Prep

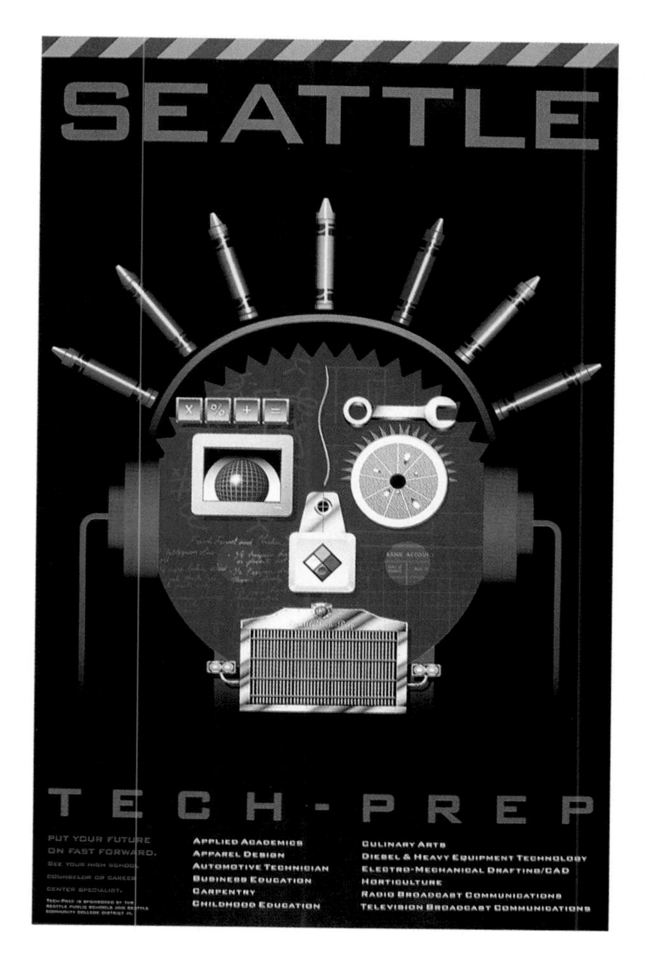

Studio Seireeni

Los Angeles, California, USA

Richard Seireeni

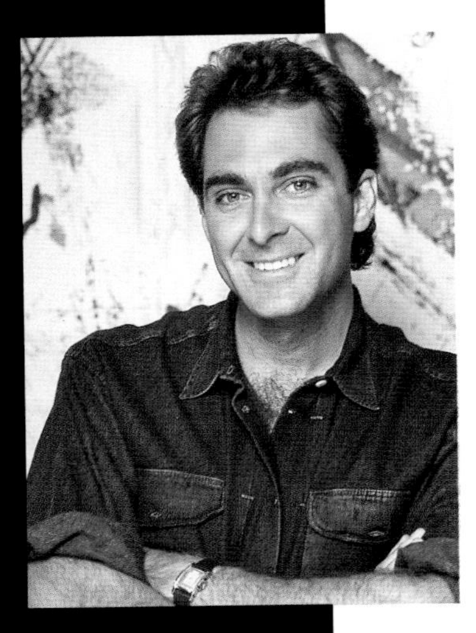

Richard Seireeni graduated from the University of Washington's Department of Architecture. He spent his graduate year in Rome and returned home to Seattle to work with the urban renewal team that restored the city's Pike Place Public Market — his first exposure to graphics. Seireeni later moved to California to work as associate art director of *Rolling Stone* magazine. Then, in the early eighties, he became art director at Warner Bros. Records. In 1984, Studio Seireeni, originally Vigon Seireeni, was founded. Today, Studio Seireeni serves a broad list of clients, from recreational parks, to apparel firms, to international legal organizations, to the world's largest sports bar.

CATALOG
Kata

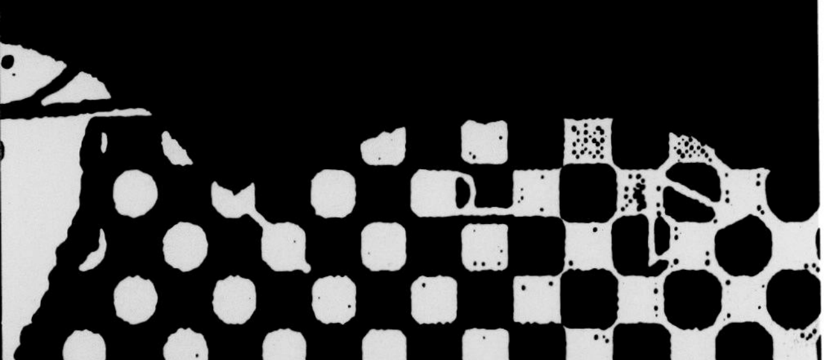

STATIONERY
Never Never Adrian

STARBRIGHT

Starbright

LOGO
BoKaos

CATALOG
Earth Life Animal Power Gotcha

CATALOG
Weavers

The Walking Store

The Walking Store

"There is no question that computers have improved the capabilities and performance of graphic designers. Speed, flexibility, economy, and the ability to see results instantly are the chief assets of computers." Richard Seireeni, however, isn't completely sure the advent of affordable graphics technology is all for the better. "On the down side, computers have opened the world of design to millions of non-designers. The result has been a flood of slick, quickly produced logos and desktop-published graphics that are drowning the truly creative work. An additional problem is that many clients now expect work quicker and cheaper than ever before. But good, original, and appropriate design still takes the same amount of research, thought, and planning. The computer has only cut time on the execution side of the design process."

Technology, according to Seireeni, is simply one interface on the way to the solution. "What computers can or cannot do depends on the operator and efficiency. Some retouching functions are still better done conventionally, like changing the shape of a hand in a photo. But moving that hand may better be done on the computer.

"In our studio, we have two primary Mac stations and two designers who constantly occupy them. Freelancers wait in line. As company owner, I use and understand the Macs the least. But I understand the principles, and I direct how a project should proceed based on that understanding. I think I'm now more of a graphics problem solver than a graphic designer. This has allowed my work to remain more flexible, less trend-specific, and more directed to client problems and needs.

"Certainly, the learning curve associated with new programs is a factor in our decision to buy and use equipment. But as the capability needs grow, we seem to find the time to learn the new stuff. With any given program, we normally only use a fraction of its full capability. And, in certain cases, we find it easier to use an outside computer service than buy a specific software to do the job ourselves."

SIGN
Wild Blue Yokohama

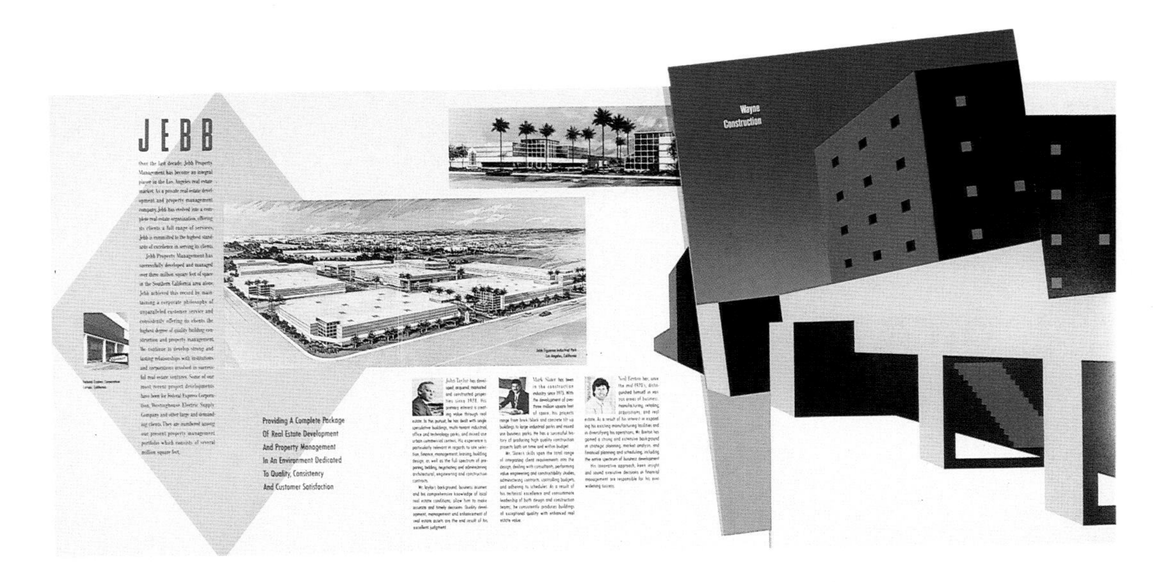

BROCHURE
Jebb-Wayne Property
Management & Development

Jayro

J A Y R O

Jayro

Tharp Did It

Los Gatos, California, USA

Rick Tharp

Mel Lindstrom

Tharp Did It is a six-person studio on the San Francisco penninsula, with an appendage in Portland, Oregon. Art director and designer Rick Tharp maintains that having control and the fun involved in doing so are the rewards of keeping the staff small. Their work has attracted such clients as Mirassou Vineyards, Hewlett-Packard, and BRIO Toys in Sweden. Tharp's posters for BRIO are part of the Smithsonian's Cooper-Hewitt Museum, and a book designed for the same client is in the permanent collection of the Library of Congress. The firm's work has been recognized by the New York and San Francisco Art Directors Clubs, the Clio's, the American Center for Design, and the American Institute of Graphic Arts, among others.

HOW

PACKAGING
Awesome Liqueur

POSTER SERIES
BRIO

PACKAGING
Massage Oil

Rick Tharp has had some success avoiding the use of computers in graphics. "I can draw a better line without a straight-edge than a computer-aided designer can," says Tharp. "I didn't say a *straighter* line — I said a *better* line."

In fact, *Ad Age* magazine referred to Tharp as a Luddite — one of a group of 19th-century workmen who destroyed labor-saving machinery as a protest. Tharp acknowledges some similarities. "I grew up as a designer in the 1970s without access to computers. I learned to articulate an idea or layout readily in a sketch. I see many designers who can't draw, and I don't think this is due to a lack of talent, but a lack of time spent studying rendering or visualization techniques. About all I see in their portfolios is layered and manipulated typography. I know typographers that can do that stuff better than the computer can."

Fire & Ice Liqueur

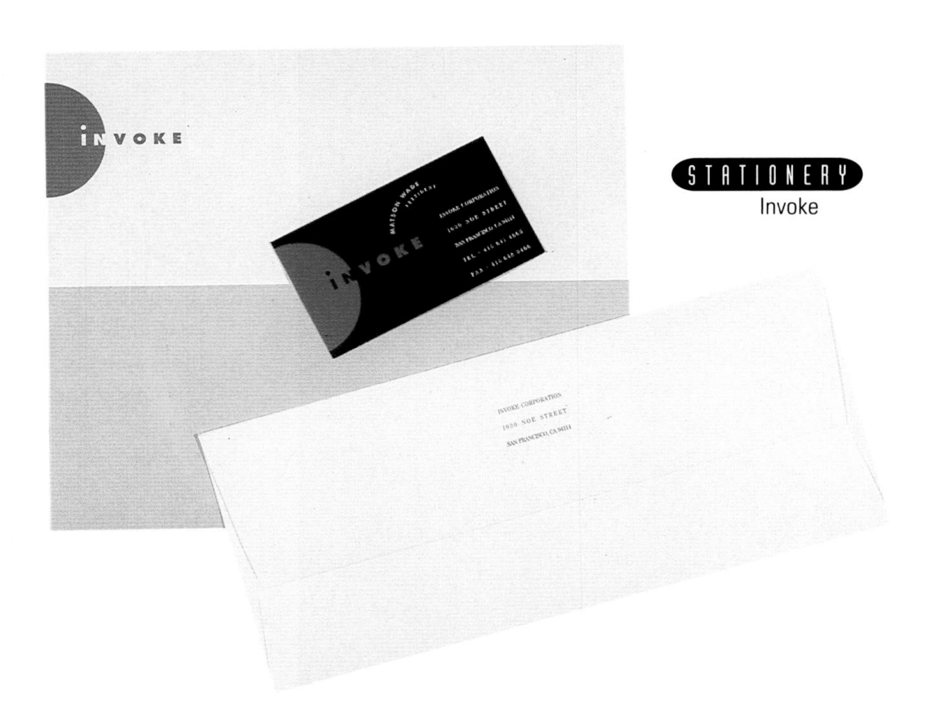

STATIONERY
Invoke

Tharp concedes a computer's value for some applications. "About half of our studio's production work is done on a Mac, but outside of our office by competent typographers and production artists, which allows us time to do what we do best. Writers or clients who supply us with text on a disk save us many hours of re-keying. But I have friends in the San Francisco design community who spend most of their time on the computer in what I consider the production phase of design. There are only 24 hours in a day and seven days a week. I prefer to use that time designing.

"In the hands of someone who truly understands typography, the computer is valuable equipment. For a designer who wants to become a typographer or a film stripper, computers are indispensable. But as far as design goes, I believe cocktail napkins are cheaper and faster than a good software program."

STATIONERY & STICKER
X-100

IDENTITY
Blackhawk Grille

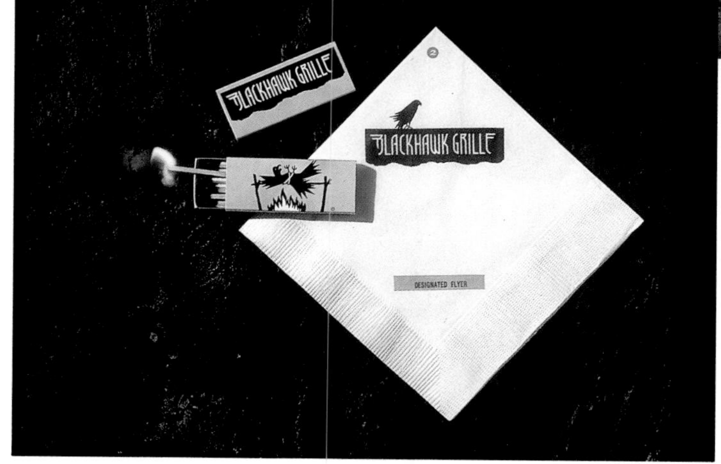

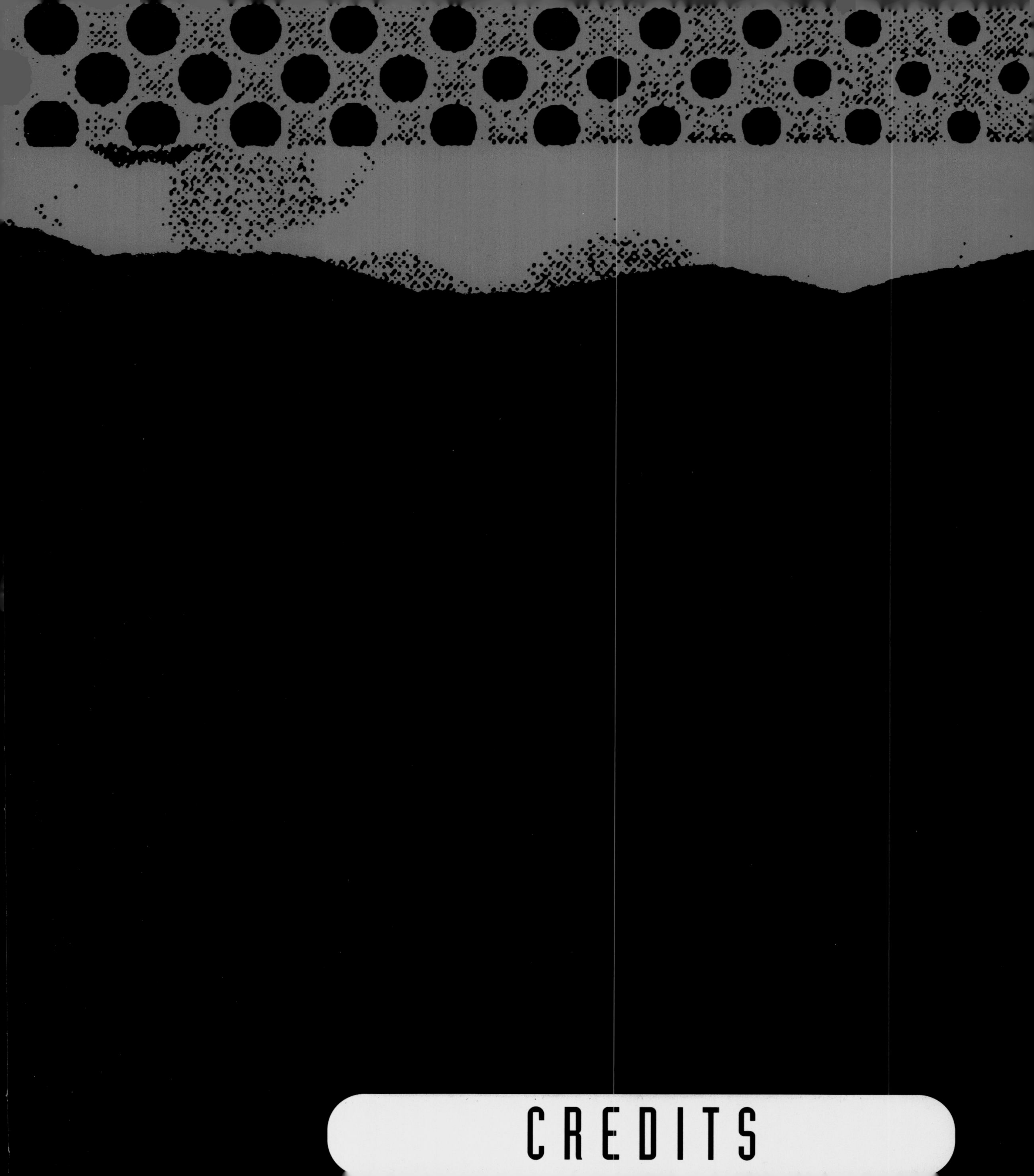

CREDITS

April Greiman, Inc.

pages 2-7

IDENTITY SYSTEM
Cerritos Center for the Performing Arts

Software: PageMaker, Illustrator
Art Director: April Greiman
Designers: April Greiman, Sean Adams
Client: Cerritos Center for the Performing Arts

SIGNAGE SYSTEM
Cerritos Center for the Performing Arts

Software: PageMaker, Illustrator, Photoshop
Art Director: April Greiman
Designers: April Greiman, Sean Adams
Client: Cerritos Center for the Performing Arts

TILE MOTIF
Cerritos Center for the Performing Arts

Software: MacDraw, Illustrator
Art Director: April Greiman
Designers: April Greiman, Michael Ellison, Sean Adams, Noreen Morioka, Elizabeth Bain
Client: Barton Myers Associates, Architects

TV IDENTITY SPOTS
Lifetime Television

Software: Photoshop, Paintbox
Art Director: April Greiman
Designers: April Greiman, Eric Martin
Photographers: April Greiman, Eric Martin
Client: Lifetime Television

POSTER
Pikes Peak Lithographing Company
(front and back)

Software: Photoshop, PageMaker
Art Director: April Greiman
Designer: April Greiman
Illustrator: April Greiman
Client: The Pikes Peak Lithographing Company

SIGNAGE
Pacific Theater

Software: PageMaker, Illustrator
Art Director: April Greiman
Designers: April Greiman, Sean Adams
Client: Pacific Theater

STUDENT WORKBOOK
From the Edge

Software: Photoshop, PageMaker, Illustrator
Art Director: April Greiman
Designers: April Greiman, Sean Adams
Writers: Margaret Reeve, Michael Rotondi
Photographers: various
Client: Southern California Institute of Architecture

Brigham Young University Graphics

pages 8-13

POSTER
Phoenix

Software: Quark
Art Director: McRay Magleby
Designer: McRay Magleby
Illustrator: McRay Magleby
Writer: Norm Darais
Client: Brigham Young University

POSTER
Peace

Software: Quark
Art Director: McRay Magleby
Designer: McRay Magleby
Illustrator: McRay Magleby
Writer: Norm Darais
Client: Brigham Young University

BROCHURE
Cryptic Hieroglyphics Spread

Software: Quark
Art Director: McRay Magleby
Designer: McRay Magleby
Illustrator: McRay Magleby
Writer: Norm Darais
Client: Brigham Young University

BROCHURE
Astronomy Spread

Software: Quark
Art Director: McRay Magleby
Designer: McRay Magleby
Illustrator: McRay Magleby
Writer: Norm Darais
Client: Brigham Young University

POSTER
Parrot

Software: Quark
Art Director: McRay Magleby
Designer: McRay Magleby
Illustrator: McRay Magleby
Writer: Norm Darais
Client: Brigham Young University

BROCHURE
Rembrandt as Printmaker

Art Director: Bruce Patrick
Designers: Bruce Patrick, Jonathan Skousen
Illustrator: Rembrandt
Photographer: David W. Hawkinson
Writers: Various
Editor: Martha M. Peacock
Client: Brigham Young University, College of Fine Arts and Communications

POSTER
Cerberus

Software: Quark
Art Director: McRay Magleby
Designer: McRay Magleby
Illustrator: McRay Magleby
Writer: Norm Darais
Client: Brigham Young University

POSTER
Fish

Software: Quark
Art Director: McRay Magleby
Designer: McRay Magleby
Illustrator: McRay Magleby
Writer: Norm Darais
Client: Brigham Young University

POSTER
AIDS

Software: Quark
Art Director: McRay Magleby
Designer: McRay Magleby
Illustrator: McRay Magleby
Writer: Norm Darais
Client: Brigham Young University

Bright & Associates

pages 14-19

PACKAGING
Darkseed Computer Software

Software: FreeHand
Art Director: Keith Bright
Designer: Mark Verlander
Illustrator: H.R. Giger
Client: Cyberdreams, Inc.

LOGO
Speedway Cafe

Software: FreeHand
Art Director: Keith Bright
Designer: Raymond Wood
Computer Designer: Bill Corridori
Illustrator: Raymond Wood
Client: Speedway Cafe

LOGO
Wok Fast

Software: FreeHand
Art Director: Keith Bright
Designer: Raymond Wood
Illustrator: Mark Verlander
Client: Wok Fast Restaurants

BROCHURES
Yonex Golf & Tennis

Software: Quark, Illustrator
Art Director: Keith Bright
Designer: Bill Corridori
Illustrator: Larry Keiser
Photographer: Rich Chou
Writers: Michelle Martino, Peter Brown
Client: Yonex Corporation

IDENTITY
MobilWorks

Software: FreeHand
Art Director: Keith Bright
Designer: Mark Verlander
Client: MobilWorks

TYPE BOOKS
Andresen Typographics

Software: Illustrator
Design Firm: Bright & Associates
Art Director: Keith Bright
Designer: Wilson Ong
Illustrators: Wilson Ong, Mark Verlander
Client: Andresen Typographics

BROCHURE
Resort at Squaw Creek

Software: Illustrator, Quark
Art Director: Keith Bright
Designers: Gabrielle Mayeur, Raymond Wood
Illustrator: Wilson Ong
Photographers: David Muench, Tom Lippert, Brent Bear, Tony Roberts, Walter Hodges
Writer: Fredrica Cooper
Client: Resort at Squaw Creek

SHOPPING BAG
Murauchi

Software: FreeHand
Art Director: Keith Bright
Designer: Il Chung
Client: Murauchi Furniture Access

MANUAL
Mitsubishi Electronic Division

Software: Quark
Art Director: Keith Bright
Designer: Bill Corridori
Writer: Ben Davidson
Client: Mitsubishi

Bruce Yelaska Design

pages 20-25

PACKAGING
Toshiba MRI

Art Director: Bruce Yelaska
Designer: Bruce Yelaska
Illustrator: Kelley Burke
Client: Toshiba America Medical Systems

CONSUMER GUIDE
Catalyst

Software: Quark, Illustrator
Art Director: Bruce Yelaska
Designers: Bruce Yelaska, Wayne Samdahl
Illustrator: Ward Schumaker
Photographers: stock
Writers: Ed Pell, Don Silvers, Barbara Gore
Client: Consumer Direct Access

LOGO
Urban Horse

Art Director: Bruce Yelaska
Designer: Bruce Yelaska
Illustrator: Bruce Yelaska
Client: Urban Horse

LOGO
GCIS

Art Director: Bruce Yelaska
Designer: Bruce Yelaska
Client: General Contractors Inspection Services (GCIS)

SIGNAGE
Cafe Toma

Art Director: Bruce Yelaska
Designer: Bruce Yelaska
Client: Cafe Toma

PLAY MONEY
Serious Fun

Art Director: Bruce Yelaska
Designer: Bruce Yelaska
Illustrator: Bruce Yelaska
Writer: Bruce Yelaska
Clients: The James H. Barry Co., Marchand Marketing, Bruce Yelaska

LOGO
Life on Earth

Art Director: Bruce Yelaska
Designer: Bruce Yelaska
Illustrator: Bruce Yelaska
Client: Bank of America

EXHIBIT
Life on Earth

Software: Quark, Illustrator
Art Directors: Bruce Yelaska, Larry Bruderer
Designer: Bruce Yelaska
Illustrator: Stephen Nash
Photographers: various
Writer: Conservation International
Client: Bank of America

TOILET SEAT
Your Future Has Past

Art Director: Bruce Yelaska
Designer: Bruce Yelaska
Writer: Bruce Yelaska
Client: AIGA, San Francisco

BROCHURE
Kohnke Printing

Art Director: Bruce Yelaska
Designer: Bruce Yelaska
Illustrators: Stanley Mouse, Alton Kelley, John Mattos, Bruce Yelaska
Photographers: Tom McCarthy, Galen Rowell
Writers: Beverly McManus, Marchand Marketing
Client: Kohnke Printing

PACKAGING
Nonni's Biscotti

Software: Illustrator, Quark
Art Director: Bruce Yelaska
Designer: Bruce Yelaska
Client: Nonni's Biscotti

Cato Design Inc.

pages 26-31

BOOK COVER
View from Australia, Japanese Version

Art Director: Ken Cato
Designer: Cato Design Inc. Pty. Limited
Client: Foliograph Publishing

SIGNAGE
Scienceworks

Art Director: Ken Cato
Designer: Cato Design Inc. Pty. Limited
Client: Museum of Victoria

PROMOTIONAL CALENDAR
Eurasia Press

Art Director: Ken Cato
Designer: Cato Design Inc. Pty. Limited
Client: Eurasia Press

PROMOTIONAL CALENDAR
Eurasia Press

Art Director: Ken Cato
Designer: Cato Design Inc. Pty. Limited
Client: Eurasia Press

LAUNCH SCULPTURES
Laminex

Art Director: Ken Cato
Designer: Cato Design Inc. Pty. Limited
Client: Laminex Industries

MAGAZINE COVER
Edge, No. 3

Art Director: Ken Cato
Designer: Cato Design Inc. Pty. Limited
Client: Cato Design Inc. Pty. Limited

WINE GIFT BOXES
Cato Design Overseas Offices

Art Director: Ken Cato
Designer: Cato Design Inc. Pty. Limited
Client: Cato Design Inc. Pty. Limited

SCULPTURE
Melbourne Olympic Bid

Art Director: Ken Cato
Designer: Cato Design Inc. Pty. Limited
Client: Melbourne Olympic Bid Candidature Committee 1996

INVITATION
Melbourne Olympic Bid

Art Director: Ken Cato
Designer: Cato Design Inc. Pty. Limited
Client: Melbourne Olympic Bid Candidature Committee 1996

CARRY BAGS
C'est La Vie

Art Director: Ken Cato
Designer: Cato Design Inc. Pty. Limited
Client: C'est La Vie, Japan

Discovery Networks Creative Services

pages 32-37

PROMOTION
It's Your World/Reach It

Software: Shima-Sieke SGX (a computer paint system)
Art Director: Larnie Higgins
Designer: Larnie Higgins
Client: The Discovery Channel

PROMOTIONAL KIT
The New Learning Channel

Software: Quark, Illustrator
Art Director: Larnie Higgins
Designers: Cathy Judd, Debbie Moses
Illustrator: McRay Magelby
Client: The Learning Channel

LOGO
To Read

Software: Illustrator
Art Director: Larnie Higgins
Designer: Larnie Higgins
Illustrator: Nip Rogers
Client: The Learning Channel

PROMOTIONAL KIT
Discovery

Software: Quark, Photoshop, Illustrator
Art Director: Larnie Higgins
Designers: Cathy Judd, Debbie Moses
Writer: Steve Lance
Client: The Discovery Channel

BROCHURE
Discovery

Software: Quark
Art Director: Larnie Higgins
Writer: Steve Lance
Client: The Discovery Channel

CLOCK
Discovery

Software: Quark, Shima-Sieke SGX
Art Director: Larnie Higgins
Client: Discovery Communications, Inc.

WINE BOTTLE
Kab´ər•na´

Software: Photoshop, Quark
Art Director: Larnie Higgins
Illustrator: David Diaz
Writer: Larnie Higgins
Client: The Learning Channel

LOGO
Discovery For Kids

Software: Fractal Painter, Photoshop
Art Director: Gil Cowley
Designer: Gil Cowley
Illustrator: Larnie Higgins
Client: The Discovery Channel

BROCHURE
The Learning Channel/WHY?

Software: Photoshop
Art Director: Larnie Higgins
Designer: Larnie Higgins
Writer: Scott Greyson
Client: The Learning Channel

BROCHURE
Get Real

Software: Quark, Illustrator
Art Director: Larnie Higgins
Photographer: Jeff O'Connor
Writer: Steve Lance
Client: Discovery Communications, Inc.

T-SHIRT
Shark Week '90

Software: Illustrator
Art Director: Larnie Higgins
Client: The Discovery Channel

BUTTONS
The Learning Channel

Software: Photoshop
Designer: Debbie Moses
Client: The Learning Channel

Earl Gee Design

pages 38-43

SOFTWARE PACKAGE
Perspective

Software: Quark, Illustrator, Photoshop
Art Director: Earl Gee
Designers: Earl Gee, Fani Chung
Illustrators: Earl Gee, David Bottoms
Writer: Bob Roblin
Client: Pensoft Corporation

TRADESHOW EXHIBIT
Chronicle Books

Software: Quark, Illustrator
Art Director: Earl Gee
Designer: Earl Gee
Photographer: Andy Caulfield
Client: Chronicle Books

ANNOUNCEMENT POSTER
Implosion Gallery

Software: Quark, TypeAlign
Art Director: Earl Gee
Designers: Earl Gee, Fani Chung
Illustrators: Earl Gee, Fani Chung
Writer: Ann Meissner
Client: San Francisco Arts Commission Gallery

SOFTWARE PACKAGING
BrushStrokes, Retrieve It!

Software: Quark, Illustrator, Photoshop
Art Director: Earl Gee
Designers: Earl Gee, Fani Chung
Illustrators: Earl Gee, David Bottoms
Writer: Susan Berman
Client: Claris Clear Choice

POSTER
Eames Lecture: "A Thousand Points of Departure . . . "

Software: Quark, Illustrator
Art Director: Earl Gee
Designer: Earl Gee
Illustrator: Earl Gee
Writer: Ralph Caplan
Printer: AR Lithographers
Client: AIGA, San Francisco

ANNUAL REPORT
Energy + Expansion + Expertise = Evolution

Software: Quark, Illustrator, PageMaker
Art Director: Earl Gee
Designers: Earl Gee, Fani Chung
Photographer: Geoffrey Nelson
Writer: Edelman Public Relations Worldwide
Client: Collagen Corporation

TRADE AD
The Standard

Software: Quark, Illustrator, PageMaker
Art Director: Earl Gee
Designer: Earl Gee
Photographer: Geoffrey Nelson
Writer: Morgan Thomas
Printer: AR Lithographers
Client: Greenleaf Medical

TRADE AD
Working Asset

Software: Quark, Illustrator, PageMaker
Art Director: Earl Gee
Designer: Earl Gee
Photographer: Geoffrey Nelson
Writer: Morgan Thomas
Printer: AR Lithographers
Client: Greenleaf Medical

TRADE AD
Network Support

Software: Quark, Illustrator, PageMaker
Art Director: Earl Gee
Designer: Earl Gee
Photographer: Geoffrey Nelson
Writer: Morgan Thomas
Printer: AR Lithographers
Client: Greenleaf Medical

Evenson Design Group

pages 44-49

COMPACT DISC COVER
Capitol - MVP

Software: FreeHand
Art Director: Stan Evenson
Designer: Glenn Sakamoto
Client: Capitol Records

STATIONERY
Radio Gabby

Software: FreeHand
Art Director: Stan Evenson
Designer: Glenn Sakamoto
Client: Radio Gabby

LOGO
Radio Gabby

Software: FreeHand
Art Director: Stan Evenson
Designer: Stan Evenson, Glenn Sakamoto
Client: Radio Gabby

LOGO
Private Exercise

Software: Illustrator
Art Director: Stan Evenson
Designer: Ken Loh
Client: Private Exercise Facilities

LOGO
BeBe & CeCe Winans

Software: FreeHand
Art Director: Stan Evenson
Designer: Stan Evenson, Glenn Sakamoto
Client: Capitol Records

PACKAGING
Front Row Series

Software: Quark
Art Director: Stan Evenson
Designer: Glenn Sakamoto
Client: Capitol Records

PACKAGING
Seiko Phone Card

Art Director: Stan Evenson
Designer: Stan Evenson
Client: Seiko

PROMOTION
AIGA/LA Freedom of Expression

Software: FreeHand
Art Director: Stan Evenson
Designer: Glenn Sakamoto
Client: American Institute of Graphic Arts, Los Angeles

CALL FOR ENTRIES
Prism Awards

Software: Illustrator
Art Director: Stan Evenson
Designers: Stan Evenson, Ken Loh
Client: Prism

KIT
Squirt Force

Software: Quark
Art Director: Stan Evenson
Designers: Stan Evenson, Sepi Banibashar
Client: American Institute of Graphic Arts, Los Angeles

PROMOTIONAL BOOKLET
Martha Productions Inc.

Software: FreeHand
Art Director: Stan Evenson
Designers: Stan Evenson, Glenn Sakamoto
Client: Martha Productions Inc., Artist Representatives

FHA Design

pages 50-55

ANNUAL REPORT
Biomolecular Research Institute

Software: Illustrator, Quark
Art Director: Richard Henderson
Designers: Richard Henderson, Keith Smith, Heather Mackenzie
Computer Operator: Chris Lambe
Photographer: supplied by client
Client: Biomolecular Research Institute

POSTER
Greenmill Dance Project

Software: Illustrator, Quark
Art Director: Richard Henderson
Designers: Keith Smith, Lee McCartney
Computer Operator: Naomi Hewitt
Photographer: Tat-Ming Yu
Client: Greenmill Dance Project

LOGO
Greenmill Dance Project

Software: Illustrator, Photoshop
Art Director: Richard Henderson
Designers: Lee McCartney, Richard Henderson
Computer Operators: Chris Lambe, Naomi Hewitt
Photographer: Tat-Ming Yu
Client: Greenmill Dance Project

STATIONERY
Laine Furnishings

Software: PageMaker
Art Director: Richard Henderson
Designers: Richard Henderson, Lee McCartney
Computer Operators: Chris Lambe, Naomi Hewitt
Client: Laine Furnishings

BROCHURE
Ansett Technologies

Software: Quark, Illustrator
Art Director: Richard Henderson
Designers: Richard Henderson, Keith Smith
Computer Operator: Naomi Hewitt
Photographer: James Cant
Client: Ansett Technologies

LOGO
Top of the Bay

Software: Illustrator
Art Director: Richard Henderson
Designers: Richard Henderson, Lee McCartney, Julia Jarvis
Computer Operators: Chris Lambe, Naomi Hewitt
Client: Top of the Bay

CLOTHING APPLICATION
Top of the Bay

Software: Illustrator
Art Director: Richard Henderson
Designers: Richard Henderson, Lee McCartney, Julia Jarvis
Computer Operators: Chris Lambe, Naomi Hewitt
Client: Top of the Bay

MENU & MATCHES
Level One

Software: Quark, Illustrator
Art Director: Richard Henderson
Designers: Richard Henderson, Julie Kemp
Computer Operator: Chris Lambe
Client: Grand Hyatt Melbourne

STOREFRONT
Australia on Collins

Software: Illustrator
Art Director: Richard Henderson
Designers: Richard Henderson, Lee McCartney
Computer Operator: Chris Lambe
Client: Australia on Collins

LOGO
Australia on Collins

Software: Illustrator
Art Director: Richard Henderson
Designers: Richard Henderson, Lee McCartney
Computer Operator: Chris Lambe
Client: Australia on Collins

LOGO
Level One

Software: Illustrator
Art Director: Richard Henderson
Designers: Richard Henderson, Julie Kemp
Computer Operator: Chris Lambe
Client: Grand Hyatt Melbourne

BROCHURE
Typo Mac

Software: Quark
Art Director: Richard Henderson
Designers: Richard Henderson, Ken Shadbolt, Keith Smith
Computer Operator: Naomi Hewitt
Photographer: Tat-Ming Yu
Client: Typographical Services

KINETIK Communication Graphics, Inc.

pages 56-61

BOOK
Herald Square

Software: PageMaker
Art Directors: Jeff Fabian, Sam Shelton, Jean Kane
Designers: Jeff Fabian, Sam Shelton, Jean Kane
Photographers: various
Writers: Stuart Miller, Peter Muller
Client: Walton Companies

INVITATION
A Votre Santé

Art Directors: Jeff Fabian, Sam Shelton, Laura Latham
Designers: Jeff Fabian, Sam Shelton, Laura Latham
Photographer: Geof Kern
Writer: Cheryl Duvall
Client: Design Industries Foundation for AIDS, D.C.

LECTURE INVITATION
Type That Talks

Art Directors: Jeff Fabian, Sam Shelton, Jean Kane
Designers: Jeff Fabian, Sam Shelton, Jean Kane
Client: Art Directors Club of Metropolitan Washington

PROMOTION
Jingle Java

Software: FreeHand, Quark
Art Directors: Jeff Fabian, Sam Shelton
Designers: Jeff Fabian, Sam Shelton, Amy Gustincic, Richard Kraus
Illustrator: Jeff Fabian
Client: KINETIK Communication Graphics

SELF PROMOTION
Leap Day

Art Directors: Jeff Fabian, Sam Shelton
Designers: Jeff Fabian, Sam Shelton, Richard Kraus
Writer: KINETIK Communication Graphics
Client: KINETIK Communication Graphics

DATABOOK
Kids Count

Software: PageMaker
Art Directors: Jeff Fabian, Sam Shelton
Designers: Jeff Fabian, Sam Shelton
Photographer: Max Hirshfeld
Writer: Judy Weitz
Client: The Annie E. Casey Foundation/Center for the Study of Social Policy

PACKAGING
A World of Animals

Software: Quark, FreeHand
Art Directors: Jeff Fabian, Sam Shelton, Jim Hiscott
Designers: Jeff Fabian, Sam Shelton, Amy Gustincic
Photographers: various
Writer: Julie Vosburgh Agnone
Client: National Geographic Society

PACKAGING
Wonders of Learning CD ROM

Software: FreeHand, Quark
Art Directors: Jeff Fabian, Sam Shelton, Jim Hiscott
Designers: Jeff Fabian, Sam Shelton, Amy Gustincic
Photographers: various
Writer: Julie Vosburgh Agnone
Client: National Geographic Society

COMPACT DISC
Interlochen Center for the Arts

Software: PageMaker
Art Directors: Jeff Fabian, Sam Shelton, Jean Kane
Designers: Jeff Fabian, Sam Shelton, Jean Kane
Photographers: Wayne and Mary Brill
Writer: Wesley Horner
Client: Interlochen Center for the Arts

KROG

pages 62-67

STATIONERY
Kratochwill Brewery

Software: Corell Draw
Art Director: Edi Berk
Designer: Edi Berk
Client: Kratochwill Brewery

BROCHURE
Vili Ravnjak: Tugomer

Software: Quark, Illustrator
Art Director: Edi Berk
Designer: Edi Berk
Photographer: Tone Stojko
Writer: MGL
Client: MGL (Town Theater of Ljubljana)

POSTER
Johann Wolfgang Goethe: Stella

Software: Quark, Illustrator
Art Director: Edi Berk
Designer: Edi Berk
Photographer: Tone Stojko
Client: MGL (Town Theater of Ljubljana)

BROCHURE
Mary Pix: Nedolzna ljubica

Software: Quark, Illustrator
Art Director: Edi Berk
Designer: Edi Berk
Illustrator: Edi Berk
Photographer: Tone Stojko
Client: MGL (Town Theater of Ljubljana)

POSTERS
Oblike 90

Software: Quark, Illustrator
Art Director: Edi Berk
Designer: Edi Berk
Client: Ministry of School and Sport, Department of Voluntary Activities for Youth

IDENTITY
Program 90

Software: Quark, Illustrator
Art Director: Edi Berk
Designer: Edi Berk
Client: Ministry of School and Sport, Department of Voluntary Activities for Youth

BROCHURE
Ephraim Kishon: Bil je skrjanec

Software: Quark, Illustrator
Art Director: Edi Berk
Designer: Edi Berk
Photographer: Tone Stojko
Client: MGL (Town Theater of Ljubljana)

BROCHURE
Luigi Pirandello: Kaj je resnica

Software: Quark, Illustrator
Art Director: Edi Berk
Designer: Edi Berk
Photographer: Tone Stojko
Client: MGL (Town Theater of Ljubljana)

BROCHURE
Industrial Design Education in the World

Software: Quark, Illustrator
Art Director: Edi Berk
Designer: Edi Berk
Photographers: Various
Writers: Various
Client: Secretariat of the 17th World Congress (ICSID), Ljubljana

Modern Dog

pages 68-73

STAFF JACKET
One Reel

Art Directors: Sheila Hughes (One Reel), Robynne Raye
Designer: Robynne Raye
Client: One Reel

POSTER
The Flying Karamazov Brothers

Software: Illustrator
Art Directors: Vittorio Costarella, Robynne Raye, Michael Strassburger
Designer: Vittorio Costarella
Illustrator: Vittorio Costarella
Client: Seattle Repertory Theatre

LEATHER PATCH
Red Eraser

Art Director: Mark Dellplain
Designer: Michael Strassburger
Client: M'otto Reddot

BROCHURE
K2 Wakeboard

Software: Quark
Art Director: Blake Lewis
Designer: Vittorio Costarella, Michael Strassburger
Writer: Blake Lewis
Client: K2 Wakeboards

UMBRELLA
Bumbershoot

Art Director: Sheila Hughs, Robynne Raye
Designer: Robynne Raye
Writer: Blake Lewis
Client: One Reel, 1992 Seattle Arts Festival

PRODUCT DESIGN
K2 Snowboards

Software: Photoshop, Illustrator
Art Director: Brent Turner, Luke Edgar, Jason Kasnitz
Designer: Michael Strassburger, Robynne Raye, Vittorio Costarella
Client: K2 Snowboards

POSTER
Lips Together, Teeth Apart

Software: Photoshop, Illustrator, PageMaker
Art Directors: Robynne Raye, Douglas Hughes
Designer: Robynne Raye
Client: Seattle Repertory Theatre

ADVERTISEMENT
Billboard Magazine

Software: Quark
Art Director: Jeri Heiden
Designer: Vittorio Costarella
Illustrator: Vittorio Costarella
Client: Warner Bros. Records

Neville Brody Studio

pages 74-79

PROMOTIONAL POSTER
Fuse 1

Software: Photoshop, Quark
Art Director: Neville Brody
Designer: Neville Brody
Client: Fontshop International, Berlin

PROMOTIONAL POSTER
The Hafler Trio/A Thirsty Fish

Software: PhotoShop, FreeHand
Designer: Giles Dunn
Client: Touch

PROMOTIONAL POSTER
Digitalogue

Software: PhotoShop, FreeHand
Art Director: Neville Brody
Designer: Neville Brody
Client: Digitalogue, Japan

PROMOTIONAL POSTER
Saiten Klänge

Software: FreeHand
Designer: Simon Staines
Client: Haus der Kulturen der Welt

PROMOTIONAL POSTER
World Street Music Festival

Software: PhotoShop, Quark
Designer: John Critchley
Client: Haus der Kulturen der Welt

PROMOTIONAL POSTER
Gespannt auf . . . /Wolfgang Leonhard

Software: Quark
Designer: Giles Dunn
Client: Kunst- und Ausstellungshalle der Bundesrepublik Deutschland

PROMOTIONAL POSTER
Gioblitz

Software: PhotoShop, Quark
Art Director: Neville Brody
Designer: Neville Brody
Client: ASICS Corporation, Japan

PROMOTIONAL POSTER
30 Posters on Environment and Development, The United Nations Rio Conference '92

Software: PhotoShop, FreeHand
Art Director: Neville Brody
Designer: Neville Brody
Client: Axis Design Rio

PROMOTIONAL POSTER
GAM

Software: PhotoShop, Fontographer
Art Director: Naomi Enami
Designer: Neville Brody
Client: •Too Corporation, Japan

Pat Taylor, Inc.

pages 80-85

QUARTERLY JOURNAL
AIGA, Fall 1990

Art Director: Pat Taylor
Designer: Pat Taylor
Writers: Nancy Rayburn, Brian Dooling, David Krohne
Client: AIGA, Washington, D.C. Chapter

QUARTERLY JOURNAL
AIGA, Winter 1991

Art Director: Pat Taylor
Designer: Pat Taylor
Writers: Nancy Rayburn, Clare Wilson, Stephen Quine, Pat Taylor
Client: AIGA, Washington, D.C. Chapter

QUARTERLY JOURNAL
AIGA, Spring 1990

Art Director: Pat Taylor
Designer: Pat Taylor
Writers: Nancy Rayburn, Clare Wilson
Client: AIGA, Washington, D.C. Chapter

QUARTERLY JOURNAL
AIGA, Summer 1990

Art Director: Pat Taylor
Designer: Pat Taylor
Writers: Nancy Rayburn, Beth Singer, Antonio Acalá, Pat Taylor
Client: AIGA, Washington, D.C. Chapter

CATALOG
The Story of Karl Stojka

Art Director: Pat Taylor
Designer: Pat Taylor
Illustrator: Karl Stojka
Photographer: Various
Writer: Dr. Sybil Milton
Client: U.S. Holocaust Memorial Council

LOGO
Wisconsin Star Publishers

Art Director: Pat Taylor
Designer: Pat Taylor
Illustrator: Pat Taylor
Client: Wisconsin Star Publishers

LOGO
Frank Evans Art Supplies

Art Director: Pat Taylor
Designer: Pat Taylor
Illustrator: Pat Taylor
Client: Frank Evans Art Supplies

LOGO
Hastings Development Corp.

Art Director: Pat Taylor
Designer: Pat Taylor
Illustrator: Pat Taylor
Client: Hastings Development Corp.

LOGO
Marvelous Books, Inc.

Art Director: Pat Taylor
Designer: Pat Taylor
Illustrator: Pat Taylor
Client: Marvelous Books, Inc.

LOGO
Isler & Isler Contractors

Art Director: Pat Taylor
Designer: Pat Taylor
Illustrator: Pat Taylor
Client: Isler & Isler Contractors

LOGO
Everly Elevator Co.

Software: Illustrator
Art Director: Pat Taylor
Designer: Pat Taylor
Illustrator: Graphics by Gallo, Washington, D.C.
Client: Everly Elevator Co.

POSTER
AIDS Education

Art Director: Pat Taylor
Designer: Pat Taylor
Illustrator: Phil's Photo, Inc., Washington, D.C.
Client: The Shoshin Society, Inc.

POSTER
Design USA Exhibit/USIA

Art Director: Pat Taylor
Designer: Pat Taylor
Illustrator: Pat Taylor
Writer: USIA
Client: United States Information Agency

POSTER
Hirshhorn Museum's 10th Anniversary

Art Director: Pat Taylor
Designer: Pat Taylor
Illustrators: Phil's Photo, Washington, D.C., Pat Taylor
Writer: Pat Taylor
Client: Hirshhorn Museum & Sculpture Garden

PeterHaythornthwaite Design Ltd.

pages 86-91

IMMERSION HEATER
Hydrocollator

Art Director: Peter Haythornthwaite
Designers: Peter Haythornthwaite, Bryn Chapple
Photographer: Bill Nichol
Client: Chattanooga Group, Inc.

CORPORATE IDENTITY
Crystalite

Art Director: Peter Haythornthwaite
Designers: Peter Haythornthwaite, Peter Roband
Photographer: Bill Nichol
Client: Crystalite NZ Ltd

IDENTITY
Crystalite

Art Director: Peter Haythornthwaite
Designers: Peter Haythornthwaite, Peter Roband
Photographer: Peter Roband
Client: Crystalite NZ Ltd

BROCHURES
N.Z. Carpet Yarn Spinners Guild

Art Director: Peter Haythornthwaite
Designers: Peter Haythornthwaite, Peter Roband
Photographer: Neil Liversedge
Client: N.Z. Carpet Yarn Spinners Guild (N.Z. Wool Board)

STUDIO STOVE
Oh Ah Stove & Tools

Art Director: Peter Haythornthwaite
Designers: Peter Haythornthwaite, Jim Griffin, Nick Moyes
Effects: metal components cut out by N.C.-controlled plasma cutter
Photographer: Neil Liversedge Client: Ipso Facto

PROMOTIONAL CATALOG
Corporate Gift

Art Director: Peter Haythornthwaite
Designers: Peter Roband, Peter Haythornthwaite
Photographers: Neil Liversedge, Bill Nichol
Writer: client
Client: Corporate Image Ltd

IDENTITY
Comset

Art Director: Peter Haythornthwaite
Designers: Peter Haythornthwaite, Peter Roband
Photographer: Bill Nichol
Writer: client
Client: Comset Ltd

CATALOG
Technicom

Software: Photoshop, PageMaker
Art Director: Peter Haythornthwaite
Designers: Peter Roband, Peter Haythornthwaite
Photographer: Neil Liversedge
Client: Technicom 2.0 Ltd

DESK ITEMS
är' ti-fakt-s

Art Director: Peter Haythornthwaite
Designers: Peter Haythornthwaite, Jim Griffin, Bryn Chapple, Michael Woods
Photographer: Bill Nichol
Client: är' ti-fakt-s Designs Ltd

PACKAGING
är' ti-fakt-s

Art Director: Peter Haythornthwaite
Designer: Peter Haythornthwaite
Photographer: Peter Haythornthwaite
Writer: Peter Haythornthwaite
Client: är' ti-fakt-s Designs Ltd

PACKAGING
Naturalis Bubble Bath

Art Director: Peter Haythornthwaite
Designer: Peter Haythornthwaite
Photographer: Bill Nichol
Writers: client, Peter Haythornthwaite
Client: Multichem Laboratories

Pinkhaus Design Corp.

pages 92-97

BOOK
American Directory of Architects

Software: Photoshop, Illustrator
Art Directors: Joel Fuller, Tom Sterling, Mark Cantor
Designer: Tom Sterling
Illustrator: Ralf Schuetz
Photographer: James Palma
Writer: Philip Smith
Client: Pinkhaus Publications, Inc.

STATIONERY
Pinkhaus Design Corp.

Software: Illustrator
Art Directors: Joel Fuller, Tom Sterling, Mark Cantor
Designers: Tom Sterling, Joel Fuller
Photographer: Gallen Mei
Client: Pinkhaus Design Corp.

PROMOTION
Gilbert Oxford

Software: Illustrator
Art Directors: Joel Fuller, Claudia DeCastro
Designers: Joel Fuller, Claudia DeCastro
Photographer: Gallen Mei
Writer: Frank Cunningham
Client: Su McGlouchlin, Gilbert Paper

COMPACT DISC
Change-It

Software: Illustrator
Art Director: Tom Sterling
Designer: Tom Sterling
Illustrator: Ralf Schuetz
Writer: Sister Red
Client: Sister Red

PACKAGING
Sister Red

Software: Illustrator
Art Directors: Tom Sterling
Designer: Tom Sterling
Illustrator: Ralph Schuetz
Photographer: Sister Red
Writer: Sister Red
Client: Sister Red

PROMOTION
Gilbert Esse

Software: Illustrator
Art Directors: Joel Fuller, Tom Sterling, Mark Cantor
Designers: Joel Fuller, Tom Sterling
Photographer: Gallen Mei
Writer: Frank Cunningham
Client: Su McGlouchlin, Gilbert Paper

BROCHURE
Rex

Software: Illustrator
Art Directors: Joel Fuller, Lisa Ashworth
Designers: Lisa Ashworth, Joel Fuller
Photographer: Michael Dakota
Writer: Frank Cunningham
Client: Steve Miller, Rex Three, Inc. (Printers and Separators)

STATIONERY
Rex

Software: Illustrator
Art Directors: Joel Fuller, Lisa Ashworth
Designer: Lisa Ashworth
Illustrator: Ralf Schuetz
Client: Steve Miller, Rex Three, Inc.
(Printers and Separators)

BROCHURE
African Sailing Safaris

Software: Illustrator
Art Directors: Joel Fuller, Claudia DeCastro
Designer: Claudia DeCastro
Photographers: Stephen Kraseman, Chuck Tocco
Writer: Frank Cunningham
Client: Vince Deely, Royal Viking Line

PACKAGING
Valentini Italian Ices

Software: Illustrator
Art Directors: Joel Fuller, Lisa Ashworth
Designer: Lisa Ashworth
Illustrator: Javier Romero
Client: Valentini Italian Specialties

Planet Design Company

pages 98-103

BROCHURE
Arlington International Racecourse Ltd.

Software: Quark, FreeHand
Art Directors: Dana Lytle, Kevin Wade
Designers: Kevin Wade, Dana Lytle
Illustrator: Aden Von Hager
Client: Arian, Lowe & Travis Advertising

POSTER
Holding Strong/Madison AIDS Support Network

Art Directors: Dana Lytle, Kevin Wade
Designers: Kevin Wade, Dana Lytle,
Erik Johnson, Tom Jenkins
Illustrator: Erik Johnson
Writer: Planet Design Co.
Client: Madison AIDS Support Network

POSTERS
Joiner Software Inc.
(now Wingra Technologies)

Software: FreeHand
Art Directors: Dana Lytle, Kevin Wade
Designer: Dana Lytle
Writer: John Anderson
Client: Joiner Software Inc.
(now Wingra Technologies)

ANNUAL REPORT
Century Communications Corporations Inc.

Software: Quark, FreeHand
Art Directors: Dana Lytle, Kevin Wade
Designers: Kevin Wade, Dana Lytle
Illustrator: Doug Edmunds
Photographer: Doug Edmunds
Client: Century Communications
Corporations Inc.

POSTER
Art of the Book

Art Directors: Dana Lytle, Kevin Wade
Designer: Dana Lytle
Client: Madison Art Center

CATALOG
Freeman Shoe Co. (FSC)

Software: Quark
Art Directors: Dana Lytle, Kevin Wade
Designer: Dana Lytle
Photographer: Mike Rebholz
Client: Freeman Shoe Co. (FSC)

POSTER
American Players Theatre 1991 Season

Software: Quark
Art Directors: Dana Lytle, Kevin Wade
Designers: Dana Lytle, Erik Johnson
Illustrator: Erik Johnson
Writer: John Anderson
Client: American Players Theatre

PROMOTIONAL BOOK
In Toto Fashion

Software: FreeHand
Concept: Dale Stenten, Katie Rowe
Art Director: Dale Stenten
Designer: Kevin Wade
Photographer: Dale Stenten
Client: Dale Stenten, In Toto Fashions

POSTER
Art in Bloom

Art Directors: Dana Lytle, Kevin Wade
Designer: Kevin Wade
Client: Madison Art Center

Quod Diseño y Marketing S.A.

pages 104-109

IDENTITY
Cava Chandon

Software: FreeHand, Illustrator, Quark
Designer: Josep Mª Trias
Client: Aferfrans, S.A.

CAMPAIGN
Universitat de Barcelona Academic Plan

Software: FreeHand, Illustrator, Quark
Designer: Josep Mª Trias
Client: Universitat de Barcelona

POSTER
Bazar Sos

Software: Illustrator, FreeHand
Designer: Josep Mª Trias
Client: Aldeas Infantiles Sos

PICTOGRAMS
Barcelona '92 Olympic Games

Software: Mc. View Colour, Illustrator,
FreeHand
Designer: Josep Mª Trias
Client: COOB '92, S.A.

SIGNAGE SYSTEM
Barcelona '92 Olympic Games

Software: Mc. View, Illustrator, FreeHand
Designer: Josep Mª Trias
Client: COOB '92, S.A.

POSTER
Official Symbol, Barcelona '92 Olympic Games

Software: Mc. View, Illustrator, FreeHand
Designer: Josep Mª Trias
Client: COOB '92, S.A.

POSTER
Barcelona '92 Olympic Games

Software: Mc. View, Illustrator, FreeHand
Designer: Josep Mª Trias
Client: COOB '92, S.A.

POSTER
La Recerca a Catalunya, Repte de Futur

Software: Illustrator, FreeHand
Designer: Josep Mª Trias
Client: Generalitat de Catalunya

POSTER
Punt de Servei

Software: Illustrator, FreeHand
Designer: Josep Mª Trias
Client: Enher

POSTER
No Fugis d'Estudi

Software: Illustrator, FreeHand
Designer: Josep Mª Trias
Client: Generalitat de Catalunya

POSTER
Cap a la Reforma

Software: Illustrator, FreeHand
Designer: Josep Mª Trias
Client: Generalitat de Catalunya

Reactor Art and Design, Ltd.

pages 110-115

POSTER
Happy Face

Software: Photoshop
Art Director: Donna Braggins
Illustrator: Louis Fishauf
Client: *Profit* Magazine

POSTER
Adobe Venus (Illustrator 4 for Windows)

Software: Illustrator
Art Director: Don Craig
Designer: Louis Fishauf
Illustrator: Louis Fishauf
Client: Adobe Systems Inc.

POSTER
Festival of Festivals 90

Software: Illustrator
Designer: Louis Fishauf
Illustrator: Louis Fishauf
Client: Festival of Festivals, Toronto

POSTER
Q.P. Doll

Software: Photoshop
Art Director: Eric Baker
Illustrator: Louis Fishauf
Client: Eric Baker Design for Presslink

POSTER
Fun with Computers

Software: Illustrator
Designer: Louis Fishauf
Client: Topix Computer Animation, Toronto

POSTER
R.E.M.

Art Director: Gail Anderson
Illustrator: Louis Fishauf
Client: *Rolling Stone* Magazine

POSTER
New Connections

Software: Illustrator, Photoshop
Art Director: Gregg Leeds
Illustrator: Louis Fishauf
Client: *Wall Street Journal*

POSTER
Mapping Software

Software: Illustrator, Photoshop
Art Directors: Robert Kanes, Mitch Shostak
Illustrator: Louis Fishauf
Client: *PC World*

POSTER
Inspirit 90

Software: Illustrator
Designer: Louis Fishauf
Client: AIGA, Birmingham

POSTER
Plague Doctor

Software: Photoshop
Illustrator: Louis Fishauf
Client: *Discover* (not published)

POSTER
Design Essentials

Software: Illustrator, Photoshop
Art Director: Eric Baker
Illustrator: Louis Fishauf
Client: Eric Baker Design for Adobe Press

POSTER
Client/Server

Art Director: Mark Koudys
Illustrator: Louis Fishauf
Client: Atlanta Art & Design for D.E.C. Canada
Publication: *Digital News*

POSTER
Power to the Planet

Software: Illustrator, Photoshop
Designer: Louis Fishauf
Client: 30 Posters on Environment & Development, Design Rio

Signals Design Group

pages 116-121

PROMOTIONAL MATERIALS
Curio Concert Series

Software: Quark, Illustrator, FreeHand
Art Director: Gus Tsetsekas
Designers: Year 1: Gus Tsetsekas, Nando DeGirolamo; Year 2: Gus Tsetsekas
Writer: David Lemon
Client: David Lemon

COMPACT DISCS
A) Silverman, B) Bach Children's Chorus, and C) Watmough

Software: Quark, FreeHand, Illustrator
Art Director: Gus Tsetsekas
Designers: A) Gus Tsetsekas, Anna Barton; B) Gus Tsetsekas, Nando DeGirolamo; C) Gus Tsetsekas, Nando DeGirolamo
Illustrator: B) Nando DeGirolamo
Calligrapher: C) Wing Shya
Photographers: A) Hans Sipma; B) John Oliphant
Clients: Robert Silverman, Vancouver Bach Children's Chorus, David Lemon

AD
Design Week

Software: Quark, FreeHand
Art Director: Gus Tsetsekas
Designer: Gus Tsetsekas
Illustrator: Nando DeGirolamo
Writer: Robyn Sossel
Client: Design British Columbia

ANNUAL REVIEW
Asia Pacific Foundation

Software: Quark
Art Director: Gus Tsetsekas
Designer: Gus Tsetsekas
Photographer: James LaBonté
Writer: Paul Grescoe
Client: Asia Pacific Foundation of Canada

PROMOTIONAL MATERIALS
1993 World Choral Symposium

Software: Quark, FreeHand, Illustrator
Art Director: Gus Tsetsekas
Designers: Gus Tsetsekas, Nando DeGirolamo, Adam Smith
Photographer: Tourism Vancouver
Writers: George Laverock, Morna Edmundson
Client: 1993 World Choral Symposium

ANNUAL REPORT
BC Central Credit Union

Software: Quark, Illustrator, FreeHand
Art Director: Gus Tsetsekas
Designers: Gus Tsetsekas, Nando DeGirolamo
Illustrator: Tannis Hopkins
Photographer: Larry Goldstein
Writer: Gayle Stevenson
Client: BC Central Credit Union

COMMEMORATIVE STAMP SERIES
Canada Post

Software: Quark, FreeHand, Illustrator, Photoshop
Art Director: Gus Tsetsekas
Designer: Gus Tsetsekas
Illustrator: Heather Price
Calligrapher: Martin Jackson
Photographer: Larry Goldstein
Client: Iain Baines, Canada Post Corporation

POLICY PAMPHLETS
Elite Insurance

Software: Quark
Art Director: Gus Tsetsekas
Designers: Gus Tsetsekas, Naomi Broudo
Illustrator: Naomi Broudo
Writer: David Young
Client: Elite Insurance

LOGO
Canadian HIV Trials Network

Software: Illustrator
Art Director: Gus Tsetsekas
Designer: Gus Tsetsekas
Client: Canadian HIV Trials Network

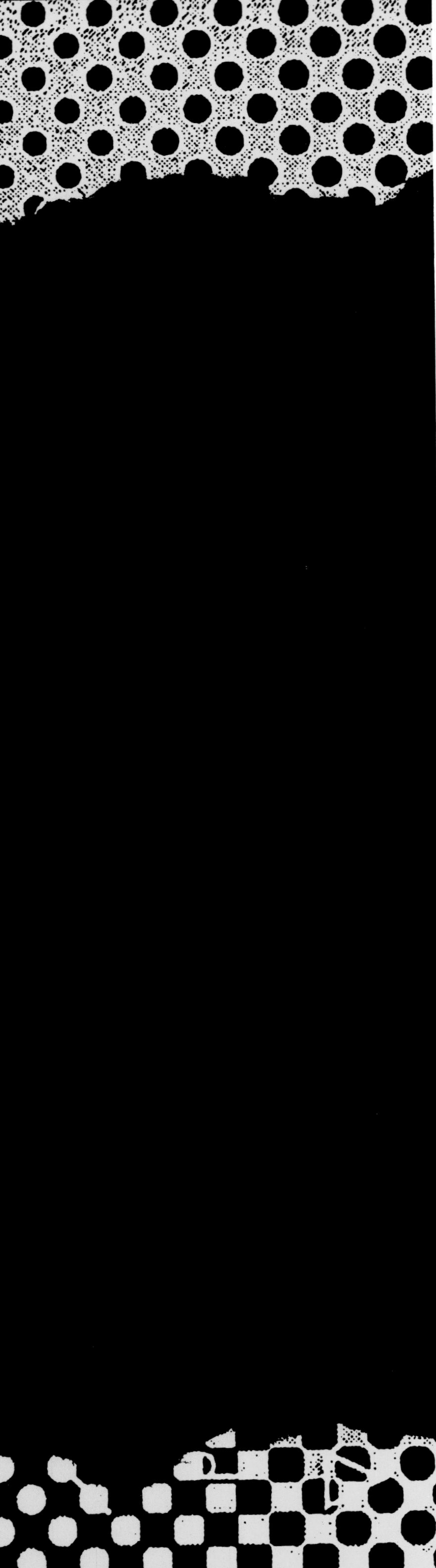

POSTER SERIES
Vancouver Opera

Software: PageMaker
Art Director: Gus Tsetsekas
Illustrator: Sandra Hoffmann
Writer: Paul Belserene
Client: Vancouver Opera

LOGO
Rouvain Recordings

Software: Illustrator
Art Director: Gus Tsetsekas
Designer: Gus Tsetsekas
Client: Robert Silverman, Rouvain Recordings

Siobhan Keaney Design

pages 122-127

CHRISTMAS CARD
The Mill

Art Director: Siobhan Keaney
Designer: Siobhan Keaney
3-D Imager/Model maker: Siobhan Keaney
Photographer: Robert Shackleton
Client: The Mill

ANNUAL REPORT
Apicorp

Software: Paintbox
Art Director: Siobhan Keaney
Designer: Siobhan Keaney
3-D Imager/Modelmaker: Siobhan Keaney
Photographer: Robert Shackleton
Client: Apicorp

BROCHURE COVER
Seymour Powell

Art Director: Siobhan Keaney
Designer: Siobhan Keaney
Client: Seymour Powell

BROCHURES & POSTERS
90-Day Access, High Rate of Interest

Software: Paintbox
Art Director: Siobhan Keaney
Designer: Siobhan Keaney
Illustrator: Siobhan Keaney
Photographer: Robert Shackleton
Client: Nationwide Building Society

ANNUAL REPORT
Apicorp

Software: Paintbox
Art Director: Siobhan Keaney
Designer: Siobhan Keaney
3-D Imager/Modelmaker: Siobhan Keaney
Photographer: Robert Shackleton
Client: Apicorp

POSTER
Daryl Jackson International, Architects

Art Director: Siobhan Keaney
Designer: Siobhan Keaney
Photographer: Robert Shackleton
Client: Daryl Jackson International, Architects

PROMOTION
Kemble Mantheakis

Art Director: Siobhan Keaney
Designer: Siobhan Keaney
Photographers: Siobhan Keaney,
Robert Shackleton
Client: Terry Kemble, Harry Mantheakis

STATIONERY
Kemble Mantheakis

Art Director: Siobhan Keaney
Designer: Siobhan Keaney
Photographers: Siobhan Keaney,
Robert Shackleton
Client: Terry Kemble, Harry Mantheakis

ALBUM COVER
What Are Dreams Made Of

Art Director: Siobhan Keaney
Designer: Siobhan Keaney
Photographer: Robert Shackleton
Client: E.G. Records, London

Spatchurst Design Associates

pages 128-133

INVITATION
The Magic of the Paris Opera

Art Director: John Spatchurst
Designer: John Spatchurst
Client: Art Gallery of New South Wales

EXHIBITION MATERIAL
Lucian Freud

Software: Quark
Art Director: John Spatchurst
Designer: John Spatchurst
Client: Art Gallery of New South Wales

EXHIBITION POSTER
the most useful Art

Art Director: John Spatchurst
Designer: John Spatchurst
Client: Art Gallery of New South Wales

STATIONERY
Various Identities

Software: Quark, Illustrator
Art Directors: John Spatchurst, Steven Joseph
Designers: John Spatchurst, Steven Joseph
Clients: various

AWARD
Workgroup of the Year

Software: Illustrator, Quark
Art Director: John Spatchurst
Designer: John Spatchurst
Manufacturer: Eckhard Reissig
Client: Sydney Electricity

ANNUAL REPORT
Westmead Hospital

Software: Quark, Illustrator
Art Director: Meryl Blundell
Designer: Meryl Blundell
Coordinator: Trish Burns
Client: Westmead and Parramatta Hospitals and Community Health Services

EXHIBITION CATALOG
Arnott's

Software: Quark
Art Director: John Spatchurst
Designer: Meryl Blundell
Writer: Charlotte Rowe
Client: The Rowland Company

BROCHURE
Australasian Wheels for the Mind

Software: PageMaker, FreeHand
Art Director: John Spatchurst
Designer: Brett Bush
Client: Australasian Apple University Consortium

LOGO PROPOSAL
Sydney Olympic 2000 Bid

Software: Illustrator
Art Director: John Spatchurst
Designer: John Spatchurst
Illustrator: Michael Fitzjames
Client: Sydney Olympic Committee

LOGO
State Library of New South Wales

Art Director: John Spatchurst
Designer: John Spatchurst
Client: State Library of New South Wales

BROCHURE
from Australia

Software: Quark
Art Director: Steven Joseph
Designer: Analiese Cairis
Editor: Sandra Symons
Client: Australia Council

Steven R. Gilmore Design

pages 134-139

POSTER
Decades

Software: FreeHand, Photoshop, EPS Exchange
Art Director: Steven R. Gilmore
Designer: Steven R. Gilmore
Photographer: Hill Peppard (large photograph)
Client: Kelly Marie Productions

POSTER
Vivienne Mackinder

Software: FreeHand, Photoshop, EPS Exchange
Art Director: Steven R. Gilmore
Designer: Steven R. Gilmore
Photographer: Cassimo Zaccaria
Client: Joico of Canada

BROCHURE
PFS Engineering

Software: FreeHand, Photoshop, EPS Exchange
Art Director: Steven R. Gilmore
Designer: Steven R. Gilmore
Photographer: Steven R Gilmore
Client: PFS Engineering

STATIONERY
PFS Engineering

Software: FreeHand, Photoshop, EPS Exchange
Art Director: Steven R. Gilmore
Designer: Steven R. Gilmore
Photographer: Steven R Gilmore
Client: PFS Engineering

MOVIE POSTER
Impolite

Software: FreeHand, Photoshop, EPS Exchange
Art Director: Steven R. Gilmore
Designer: Steven R. Gilmore
Client: Massey Productions

POSTER
Visual Aid

Software: FreeHand, Photoshop, EPS Exchange
Art Director: Steven R. Gilmore
Designer: Steven R. Gilmore
Illustrator: Steven R. Gilmore
Client: Oakridge Shopping Centre

PROMOTIONAL CARD
"Feed Your Head"

Software: FreeHand, Photoshop, EPS Exchange
Art Director: Steven R. Gilmore
Designer: Steven R. Gilmore
Illustrator: Steven R. Gilmore
Client: SRG Design

PROMOTIONAL CARD
"I had too much to dream last night"

Software: FreeHand, Photoshop, EPS Exchange
Art Director: Steven R. Gilmore
Designer: Steven R. Gilmore
Client: SRG Design

PROMOTIONAL CARD
"taste the whip in love not given lightly"

Software: FreeHand, Photoshop, EPS Exchange
Art Director: Steven R. Gilmore
Designer: Steven R. Gilmore
Photographer: Betty Page Photographs By Paula and Irving Klaw (circa 1954)
Client: SRG Design

PROMOTIONAL CARD
Rose and Thorn

Software: FreeHand, Photoshop, EPS Exchange
Art Director: Steven R. Gilmore
Designer: Steven R. Gilmore
Illustrator: Steven R. Gilmore
Client: SRG Design

Studio M D

pages 140-145

ILLUSTRATION
Aldus Fetch

Software: FreeHand, Photoshop
Art Director: Don Bergh
Illustrators: Glenn Mitsui, Randy Lim, Jesse Doquilo
Client: Aldus Corporation

HOLIDAY SCULPTURE
Sea-Tac International Airport

Software: FreeHand
Art Directors: Jesse Doquilo, Randy Lim, Glenn Mitsui
Designer: Jesse Doquilo
Client: Port of Seattle

POSTER
The First Trapeze Awards

Software: FreeHand, Photoshop, Design Painter
Art Directors: Glenn Mitsui, Jesse Doquilo, Randy Lim
Designer: Jesse Doquilo
Illustrator: Glenn Mitsui
Writers: Alex duMauriee, Claudia Meyer-Newman
Client: AIGA, Seattle

USER'S GUIDE
Acropolis Accounting Software

Software: FreeHand, Photoshop
Art Directors: Randy Lim, Glenn Mitsui, Jesse Doquilo
Designer: Randy Lim
Photographer: Henrik Kam
Client: Acropolis Software

ILLUSTRATION
HOW Business Annual '93

Software: FreeHand, Photoshop, Fractal Design Painter
Art Directors: Tony Gable, Glenn Mitsui
Designers: Tony Gable, Glenn Mitsui
Illustrator: Glenn Mitsui
Client: *HOW Magazine*

POSTER
Tony Gable and 206

Software: Photoshop
Art Directors: Tony Gable, Glenn Mitsui
Designers: Tony Gable, Glenn Mitsui
Illustrator: Glenn Mitsui
Client: Jaz Pen Productions

POSTER
Talk 'n Trash

Software: FreeHand
Art Director: Rick Hess
Designer: Rick Hess
Illustrator: Glenn Mitsui
Client: Washington State Department of Ecology

POSTER
Seattle Tech Prep

Software: FreeHand, Photoshop
Art Directors: Glenn Mitsui, Sharon Nakamura
Designer: Sharon Nakamura
Illustrator: Glenn Mitsui
Client: Seattle Public Schools & Seattle Community Colleges

Studio Seireeni

pages 146-151

CATALOG
Kata

Art Director: Romane Cameron
Designer: Romane Cameron
Illustrator: Romane Cameron
Photographer: Amedeo
Writer: Romane Cameron
Client: Wilshire Designs

STATIONERY
Never Never Adrian

Software: FreeHand
Art Director: Richard Seireeni
Designer: Brian Burchfield
Client: Never Never Adrian

LOGO
Starbright

Software: FreeHand
Art Director: Richard Seireeni
Designer: Romane Cameron
Illustrator: Romane Cameron
Client: Starbright Foundation

LOGO
BoKaos

Software: FreeHand
Art Director: Richard Seireeni
Designer: Romane Cameron
Illustrator: Romane Cameron
Client: BoKaos

CATALOG
Earth Life Animal Power Gotcha

Art Director: Richard Seireeni
Designer: Richard Seireeni
Photographer: Peggy Sirota
Client: Gotcha

CATALOG
Weavers

Art Director: Richard Seireeni
Designer: Richard Seireeni
Photographer: Dave Jensen
Client: Weavers

LOGO
The Walking Store

Software: FreeHand
Art Director: Richard Seireeni
Designer: Romane Cameron
Illustrator: Romane Cameron
Client: The Walking Company

STOREFRONT
The Walking Store

Software: FreeHand
Art Director: Richard Seireeni
Designer: Romane Cameron
Illustrator: Romane Cameron
Client: The Walking Company

SIGN
Wild Blue Yokohama

Art Director: Richard Seireeni
Designers: James Pezzullo, Jay Vigon
Clients: N.K.K. Steel, Creative Intelligence Assoc.

BROCHURE
Jebb-Wayne Property Management & Development

Art Director: Richard Seireeni
Designer: Richard Seireeni
Illustrator: Tim Clark
Writer: Richard Seireeni
Client: Jebb-Wayne Property Management

STORE INTERIOR
Jayro

Art Director: Richard Seireeni
Designer: Romane Cameron
Illustrator: Romane Cameron
Client: Jun Co., Ltd.

LOGO
Jayro

Software: FreeHand
Art Director: Richard Seireeni
Designer: Romane Cameron
Illustrator: Romane Cameron
Client: Jun Co., Ltd.

Tharp Did It

pages 152-157

MAGAZINE COVER
HOW

Designer: Rick Tharp
Illustrator: Rick Tharp
Client: F&W Publishing

PACKAGING
Awesome Liqueur

Software: Illustrator, Dimensions
Agency: Beeline Group
Art Directors: Rick Tharp, Charles Drummond
Designer: Rick Tharp
Illustrator: Steve Lyons
Writer: Charles Drummond
Client: Hiram Walker

POSTER SERIES
BRIO

Designers: Rick Tharp, Thom Marchionna
Illustrators: Rick Tharp, Thom Marchionna
Writer: Jane Krejci
Client: BRIO Scanditoy, Sweden

PACKAGING
Massage Oil

Designers: Jana Heer, Colleen Sullivan, Rick Tharp
Photographer: Kelly O'Connor
Client: Service Through Touch

PACKAGING
Fire & Ice Liqueur

Agency: Beeline Group
Art Director: Rick Tharp
Designers: Jean Mogannam, Rick Tharp
Illustrators: John Mattos (fire and ice), Rick Tharp (penguin and devil)
Client: Hiram Walker

STATIONERY
Invoke

Software: FreeHand, Quark
Designers: Rick Tharp, Jean Mogannam
Typographer: z typography
Client: Invoke Software

STATIONERY AND BUMPER STICKER
X-100

Designers: Rick Tharp, Kim Tomlinson
Client: Emmis Broadcasting

IDENTITY
Blackhawk Grille

Art Director: Rick Tharp
Designers: Jana Heer, Jean Mogannam, Rick Tharp, Kim Tomlinson
Interior Design: Engstrom & Hofling
Client: California Cafe Restaurant Corporation

1.31.94 pub $39.95 #56167